HOME SWEET
Fishbowl

Confessions of a Minister's Wife

HOME SWEET

Fishbowl

Denise Turner

WORD BOOKS
PUBLISHER
WACO, TEXAS

HOME SWEET FISHBOWL: CONFESSIONS OF A MINISTER'S WIFE

ISBN 0-8499-0301-7
Library of Congress Catalog Card Number: 81-71500
Printed in the United States of America

To
REVIS AND BECKY,
who ate a lot of *Hamburger Helper*
so that Mommy could follow some dreams

Contents

Preface

—Over seventy-five ministers' wives from many different denominations were interviewed during the researching of this book. These women reside in various parts of the country. Some are from large city churches, while others are involved in suburban churches or in small rural ones. Some chose to remain anonymous, but not all. A few are very well-known. Most are not.

—Three different questionnaires were used in conducting the interviews. Most of the interviews were conducted by mail, although some were conducted in person and others by telephone. The results were used as background study for this book and are referred to throughout the text. The general conclusions I have drawn about ministers' wives are based on these interviews and on the contact I have had with ministers' wives through the years.

—Some of my general statements about ministers' wives could probably be applied to ministers' husbands, too. However, the major thrust of the book is the minister's wife. There are three basic reasons for this. First, there are still many more of them in the world. Second, few research studies have thus far been centered around male spouses of ministers. And third, I am a minister's wife; and the book is written from my point of view.

—In this book, for convenience sake (not for the purpose of either condemning or condoning male/female issues), the masculine pronoun is used in reference to God.

—Many thanks to (in alphabetical order) Vern Adams, for attending law school; Jerry Arnold, for being my one-man fan club in my early days of writing; Jo Ann Borland, who baby-sat for me at stranger hours than any sane person would ever have agreed to; Katheryn Greaney, who has been waiting a long time to say she taught an author how to write; John Krier, for sending us off in love; Veronica Meyer and the nursery school staff, for giving peace to a working woman's mind; Larry Potts, for putting up with a silly little church kid who would have done anything to avoid growing up and marrying a minister; Bob Shearer, who restored my faith in ministers; the Solo Flight class, for caring; and G. Walter Weber, for saying, "Why not?" Thanks also to Dad, for passing along to me a gene for a very weird sense of humor; Mom, for once persuading Santa Claus to bring me a toy typewriter; Great Grandma, who taught me how to be a kid and who almost lived to see this book in print; Uncle Bud, who understood the significance of my college degree; and my two best friends, my husband and daughter, to whom this book is dedicated... and thanks to the many ministers' wives who shared their deepest feelings with me and to all the other special people who helped and encouraged me along the way.

Introduction

I was sorting through the piles of towels and bathrobes, fully aware of the fact that a real shepherd wouldn't be caught dead in orange terrycloth, when the new little girl asked me if she could be Mary's helper in the nativity drama. "What do you mean, honey?" I asked her gently. "What would Mary's helper do?" The small child looked at me solemnly and said, "Somebody has to carry the diaper bag with the Pampers, don't they?"

How quickly our world is changing! Disposable diapers are just one tiny part of the total picture. The hydrogen bomb wasn't even invented when I was born—and I still don't know how we got from 10:30 P.M. dorm hours to quickie abortions so fast. Even male and female roles are in constant flux in our society, while new values and attitudes are springing up almost as rapidly as fast food stands. Nevertheless, for better or worse, it is into this kind of world that I must hurl my plans and hopes and dreams for my life... with my husband... a minister of God.

Yes, I married the minister, and I do experience life in a very unique way because of it. Most of the time I'm glad this is true. Whenever I'm not, I tell myself that my life is filled with lots of valuable learning experiences; and, more often than not, it really is. During the past few years, for instance, I have learned (sometimes the hard way) that a viable ministry in today's world is partly dependent upon one's ability to cope with the many changes around him.

Take, for example, the twentieth-century lifestyle. Half of the people in today's world are on hold, and the other half can't find a parking place. Most of them are suffering from jet lag too. "How could any minister's wife ever relate to a world full of people like that without moving beyond impromptu visits and Thursday afternoon tea parties?" I finally asked myself. It turned out to be a very freeing question. For I've always felt uncomfortable popping in on people anyway, and I've never been able to pour tea anywhere near the cup. I figure, therefore, that I must be able to do some other things better. And maybe that is why, clammy handshakes and soggy teabags aside, I feel so ridiculously excited about being the wife of a minister in today's world. Maybe that is why I feel that my range as a minister's wife is wider today than it has ever been before.

Of course, there are many ministers' wives, even now, who insist that they are not allowed to find out what they can do. Such women say that they are being buried under a mountain of stereotypes—expected to be sweet little wallflowers who can cook like Julia Child and smile like Miss America. They explain that, in order to keep their husbands in the pulpit, they are forced to act out a collection of "old ministers' wives' tales" that no longer fit. As a result, they feel resentful, isolated, and helpless.

There is a flip side to this story though, because there are lots of ministers' wives in today's world who are mustering up the courage to reject all those stereotypes. These women are struggling to define their own roles in the church, refusing to be poured into molds, and dealing with the responsibilities and stresses of the ministry in new ways. (Hello? A call to the ministry? It's for you, dear.) What sort of fate is in store for this kind of woman? What kind of future can she look forward to?

--

Some individuals say that a minister's wife who carves out her own niche can expect to be hailed as a courageous trailblazer. Others hint that she is headed toward a burning stake. I, personally, tend to believe that the truth lies somewhere between these two extremes. For, while it is true that some people do come unglued when they encounter an individualist in a parsonage, many other people don't seem to mind at all. Perhaps there was a time when they would have minded, but that was back when everyone knew exactly what the minister's wife was supposed to be like. No one seems to be quite sure anymore.

Does this mean that we are on the brink of a liberation movement among ministers' wives? Possibly of sorts, but so far no one is burning navy blue dresses or staging sit-ins at men's breakfasts. Rather, we are simply seeing more and more ministers' wives who say, "Don't call me a minister's wife; I'm the wife of a man who just happens to be a minister." We are seeing more and more ministers' wives who go to work instead of to circle meetings. And we are seeing more and more ministers' wives who are so acutely aware of the reality of divorce in the ministry that they are searching for ways to keep from being next.

Clearly, there are some interesting things happening in the church, and in the parsonage, right now. The idea of blending that fact with the fact that we Christians serve an unchanging God may sound a bit sacrilegious to some people, but large numbers of ministers' wives don't see it that way. One, for instance, who has been happily married to her minister for fifty-two years, was quick to explain why she urges people to let go of the outdated expectations that have traditionally been thrust upon the minister's wife. She said it this way:

Like so many other matters in the church, we seem to hang onto ideas that have long since passed out just because we think things in the church "don't change." It is one of our greatest evils. The Old Testament is sure proof of the fact that although God does not need to change, the ideas about him and human understanding of him do change very considerably—thank goodness. What the prophets said about God was very different from some of the early conceptions. And then what Jesus said was way beyond the prophets' conception. I firmly believe that in our own day we may be able to arrive at some deeper understanding of what Jesus was trying to give us.

Are today's ministers' wives headed toward a deeper understanding of their roles, of their identities, of the God whom they and their husbands serve? What impact is today's minister's wife having on the church? What impact is she having on the world? And how many of us are truly aware of what is going on behind the scenes in our churches today?

1.

The Person-to-Person Call

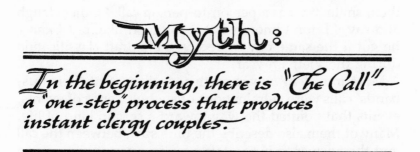

Myth:

In the beginning, there is "The Call"— a "one-step" process that produces instant clergy couples.

A minister can have flat feet, a bald head, a pot belly, and maybe even bad breath; but he will never make it to the first pulpit committee if he doesn't have "The Call." Yes, the call is definitely the prerequisite. Everyone agrees with that. Describing the call, however, is not such an easy task. For example . . . the Apostle Paul got it on the road to Damascus, and it came through loud and clear; but Samuel had to hear it three times and then seek consultation before he even realized what it was. It was compelling enough to persuade Peter and Andrew to walk away from their jobs, and it was extraordinary enough to cause Moses to talk to a bush. Jeremiah was young when he received it;

Abraham was old. . . . "The Call"—a very difficult thing to describe.

None of the ministers I know ever heard a booming voice from heaven, but all of them assure me that they have been distinctly called into the ministry. No one is arguing with them about it either, for you can question your minister's sermons and possibly even his sanity; but disputing God's call to him is very risky business. Perhaps that is why so many lay people think of God's call to the ministry as a rather mystical, somewhat vague, often confusing concept. Even ministers' wives aren't always sure how to explain their husbands' calls. "Ask him," some of them smile. "It was a person-to-person call." Others laugh and say, "I don't know what it sounded like, but I know he got it the same day he received his draft classification during the Vietnam War."

Most ministers' wives seem to believe that their husbands' calls were culminations of a whole series of events, events that pointed the way toward a certain kind of life. Many of them also describe the time span between the call and the answer to it as a fairly bumpy period of ups and downs, doubts and questions, struggles and fears. Such descriptions, of course, are far removed from the way in which Hollywood might portray a call from God. No harp-strumming angels, no soothing violin music, not even a tiny flash of streak lightning. But most of the time, as Walter Cronkite so aptly put it, "That's the way it is." And marriage often makes things even more complicated.

Would You Like to Leave a Message?

When a minister chooses a partner, when the two become one, then a new question arises: Does the call extend to the minister's wife too; does it become a station-to-station call at that point? This is a very complex question. For, while some of today's ministers' wives do feel called to participate in their husbands' ministries, there are large numbers of them who balk at the idea of the divinely hand-picked minister's wife. "We honestly wanted to marry lawyers," they may quip, "and besides, we can't believe anyone would actually set out to marry a man who will never be able to afford a Mediterranean cruise."

Many ministers' wives say that they simply married the men they love and that they never did and never would marry a profession as opposed to a person. "But if you had it to do over again," I asked a number of them, "would you still marry a minister?" The responses were interesting. "Not just any minister," one said, "but if he were Allen, I would." Another replied, "I would marry *this* minister again, because I fell in love with him, not his job or calling." And a third added, "Yes, if I loved the man, but I would consider his choice of the ministry one of the minuses in the relationship."

Still, the majority of ministers' wives do seem to feel that their clergy marriages fit within the framework of God's plan for their lives, and many of them also say that they have received different kinds of calls from God. Some, for example, talk about feeling called into various vocations or lifestyles. Others feel called into specific roles or areas of service. They appear to have no problem with the idea of calls as such. Rather, their problem is with the idea that the act of marrying a minister bestows upon a woman any sort of professional status that she has not already earned for herself.

The Trek Begins

How, then, does a woman earn her own status and also remain true to her vow to help and undergird her minister husband? Must she purchase a shiny new spinet, memorize the right how-to book, choose the correct brand of tooth polish? Some people seem to think so, but I don't see too many women rushing out to enroll in refresher classes for ministers' wives. In fact, the seminary my husband attended didn't even offer the basic course: "How to be an Ex officio Member of Women's Groups, 101." I had no real mentors either and only one or two role models who could be considered adequate endorsements for life in the manse. I never even had a guardian angel who took me aside and explained how to be a good mediator in the church kitchen.

As a result of all this, I started to feel apprehensive about my future fairly early in my marriage. There was nowhere for me to go to learn how to be a minister's wife, so I began to fear that I might not be suited to be one at all. By that time, though, I *was* a minister's wife, ready or not; and, like any other rational newlywed, I politely accepted my new title mostly because I was sure that I could live on love anyway. I certainly had no intention of cluttering up my mind with the problems I might have to face during my husband's ministry. I was much too busy having fun and playing house.

Later, when I came down to earth, it dawned on me that the house I was playing in might someday be a parsonage. (We were still living in an apartment at that time.) I also realized that I might not be cut out to live in one. In fact, I didn't really feel like a minister's wife at all; and I couldn't figure out why. Maybe I had expected to find a shortcut, an easy way to make peace with my role. Or maybe I had assumed that saying "I do" to a man of the cloth would instantly transform me into that strong, silent minister's wife I had seen gliding around on that late night TV movie.

I should have known better. For, instant soup and instant photographs notwithstanding, everything in life is certainly not instant. Take embracing the Christian faith for example. It doesn't make one instantly godly. There are still the hang-ups to wrestle with and the worries to assuage and the "fear and trembling" that is an integral part of it all. A new Christian always begins his pilgrimage just as he is. It should not have surprised me, therefore, to begin my life as a minister's wife in precisely that same place. And yet, it did surprise me. I had no idea how much ministerial underwear I would have to wash before I would discover what it actually means—and doesn't mean—to be the minister's wife.

Needless to say, I made my adjustments to married life very gradually. One day I faced the fact that I hardly knew how to boil water, much less cook the best fried chicken in the parish. Another day (after having paid many visits to the Colonel), I began to see how unnecessary it is for a minister's wife to live a life that is always finger-licking good. Still, I don't regret being a late bloomer, for, by the time I made my discoveries, I was ready to accept them. I was even ready to admit that I could have played the old minister's wife game forever and I would never have earned my Super Minister's Wife merit badge anyway. I simply don't possess any of the accepted qualities. I never did. For a long time, in fact, I didn't even know what they were.

I had certainly not been required to demonstrate any musical talent when I applied for a license to marry a minister. I didn't even have to pray out loud in front of the county clerk. Later, of course, I did hear that piano-playing could be a real plus; and I promptly brushed up on my scales. But my church piano debut was about as uninspiring as the sermon my husband wrote during a Super Bowl game; and I soon knew that I had only two choices left. I could either play loudly and pretend not to hear the E sharps, or I could carve out my own special niche in the church. Like many of my contemporary peers, I decided that the latter approach would be better; but also like many of my contemporary peers, I eventually found out that such a path, if one allows it to be so, can be paved with many tears.

On Having "Great Expectations"

Lots of people believe that the most difficult problems in the parsonage are caused by unrealistic expectations, and many ministers' wives do admit that they began their marriages with very unrealistic ones. Some say that they, themselves, expected their husbands to be perfect, at least on occasion—and certainly to be far above leaving grimy rings around the bathtub! Other women explain that they expected to be able, as ministers' wives, to personally lead masses of people to the Lord. "I don't know why I expected that," one minister's wife sighed, "because I couldn't even remember the four spiritual laws before I got married." Many ministers' wives also say that they had starry-eyed visions of large churches, beautiful homes, celebrated husbands, and lots of close, supportive friends in the church—home sweet home next door to church sweet church, one of the most popular of the make-believe worlds.

Numbers of ministers' wives, when they look back over the years, talk about how detrimental their expectations were. Take, for example, the women who expected to be good ministers' wives (instead of good wives). Many of them didn't get started down the right road until after they had stumbled down several wrong ones. And some of the ministers' wives who fully expected to use their true gifts in the church were gradually discouraged from ever doing so because they were never asked to work with anyone over the age of two.

Perhaps, then, it is best to be like the young woman who said, "I have no clear cut picture of myself filling the role of minister's wife, so I'm open for anything."

Perhaps. And yet, there is probably nothing wrong with a minister's wife having some expectations, as long as she is willing to take the responsibility for making them happen. She could expect, for instance, to grow spiritually in her church—as long as she understands that she is the one who must make it so. Or, she could expect to be at peace with herself and her role—as long as she understands that peace is always an inside job.

Lots of ministers' wives eventually do come to terms with their expectations and realizations. They do finally create their own spots in the church, and they actually begin to enjoy filling them. Unfortunately though, as soon as they get to that point, it is often time to move on. For a call to the ministry is not the only type of call a clergyman can receive. He can also be called to a new church, and the call to a new church is the kind of call that can be extended to a minister many times during his life—too many times according to some ministers' wives.

Whither Thou Goest

Granted, there are those ministers' wives who actually thrive on moving to a new church. Such women seem to have been born with an extra mobility gene. They always keep a permanent stock of packing crates tucked away in their attics; and they are ready, at the drop of a choir robe, to break the ties that bind. Other ministers' wives, however, can't even stand to look at a picture of a moving van. These women do everything possible, short of offering to pay off a denominational executive, to insure that their husbands will be among the chosen few who spend forty years in one church.

Most of us probably fall somewhere in between. I, for instance, never had any real aspirations about being in any one church forever. I never expected to get one of those long, strange-looking "Perfect Attendance at Sunday

School" pins (the kind where you add a shiny silver bar every year until you either die of old age or topple over from the weight of the thing). Instead, I have always figured that the ministry, not unlike many of today's professions, could easily involve moving on from time to time; and I have always been prepared to live with whatever inconvenience that might entail.

On the other hand though, I can certainly understand why a large number of ministers' wives list "moving" under both the positive and the negative aspects of the ministry. For, while meeting new people can be fun, there is definitely a minus side to this experience too. Many of today's ministers' wives have successful careers of their own to consider, for example. And, although immediate acceptance into a new community can be a real plus, there is something very bittersweet about experiencing any of life's little "dyings" (waving good-bye to a houseful of memories, consoling uprooted children, etc.). Add to all of this the additional pressures involved in dealing with church pulpit committees, and you have the makings of a real Excedrin headache.

Next Question, Please

Ah yes. The pulpit committee. How prepared I thought I was for my first meeting with one, and why shouldn't I have felt that way? I already knew everything there was to know about job interviews, didn't I? My husband and I had held all sorts of positions throughout college and graduate school, hadn't we? Why shouldn't I have assumed that we could sail smoothly through any pulpit committee interview?

But all of my assumptions couldn't have been more wrong; and I have never been able to figure out why. I think, however, that it might have something to do with the fact that pulpit committee members are not usually professional personnel people, thus making it hard to decide exactly how to relate to them. If you try to think of them as professional Christians, for example, you find that you have no biblical backing for such a misnomer. And if you decide to look at them as homiletic experts or semi-celestial messengers of God, you are bound to walk into the interview and be introduced to at least one eighty-year-old lady in pedal pushers.

I now believe that no one can ever fully prepare himself for those first meetings with church pulpit committees. During one of them, in fact, I was even asked if I thought it would be best for a minister to live downtown among "street people," even though his congregation doesn't, so that his home could be a refuge of sorts. It turned out to be a very loaded question, and at that time I hadn't even worked through my fantasies about cute little parsonages with white picket fences and yards full of daisies. I was, needless to say, speechless.

I was also speechless when I tried to ask my first pulpit committee a question about salary. For, like so many other people, I was afraid to mention the word *money* in such a setting. Not because of my scriptural precedents, but because I didn't know how any of the committee members interpreted scripture. Thus, on several occasions, I eventually fell into the trap of trying to second-guess my interviewers, of bouncing back the answers I thought everyone wanted to hear. And, by the end of those sessions, I generally found myself wondering if the call to a church ever really comes from God at all.

Approach #1: Hang Loose

Since those days I have done a little research into the matter, and I now know that there are many possible approaches (some good, some bad) that a minister and his wife can take when they face a pulpit committee. One possibility: they can try to keep the tone light and witty and then take their chances—like that friend of mine who was asked if he believed in the virgin birth. Having just spent a whole semester in seminary studying the theological implications of that issue, he was less than excited at the prospect of reducing an entire body of knowledge into a thirty-second reply. So, he just laughed and said, "No." Then, after a long and very uncomfortable pause, he added, "But I believe in the virgin conception." Unfortunately, the other people in the room hadn't taken the same course he had taken; and they were not amused.

Approach #2: Charge!

A second approach involves selling the committee on oneself and, thus, turning the interview into a sort of political campaign. This method probably evolved out of the idea that a person has a responsibility to promote himself—or out of the belief that too many Christians carry the fine art of humility to unnecessary extremes. At any rate, it is very easy to overdo this approach. Some people, in fact, greet pulpit committees with enough enthusiasm to lead an entire country into battle; and the result is usually fairly predictable. Any perceptive committee members are left wondering how anyone with that much excess energy could ever bring tranquility to a church full of people who argue about where to place the flowers on the communion table.

Approach #3: Take Me or Leave Me

A third approach, and probably a more promising one, is the "be yourself" approach. The underlying assumption here is that the people on a pulpit committee are simply that—people—and that most of them are also compassionate Christian people who are trying their best to hear

God's voice amid the rumble of the custodian's lawn mower outside. So, the interviewee merely relaxes and lets people see the real human being behind the façade; and then he hopes that it will be enough. When it isn't, I suppose he can take some comfort in the fact that ministers, through the years, have made excellent door-to-door salesmen.

Often though, with a little luck, a lot of prayer, and a pulpit committee that is reasonably good at matching ministers to churches, a minister's wife does find the fickle finger of fate pointed in her family's direction. Her husband does get the church's call. By that time, of course, she is too exhausted with the whole thing to even think about moving; but she has to start packing anyway.

Back on I-75

Some women find the task of moving more disruptive than other women do. I, personally, always thought of myself as one of the calmer types, until our last move, that is. It was, not coincidentally, our first move involving an infant. . . . Yes, I'll always remember that particular move as the one that turned my postpartum depression into the longest one on record. The baby was sick with a fever. Our new all-electric home had no electricity. There was mud from the construction, and there were leaks from an untightened water valve. By the time the moving van pulled out of our lumpy, unpaved driveway, my husband, my daughter, and I looked as if we had just stepped out of a situation comedy—except for the fact that no one was laughing.

A few weeks later, when I began to think again, I started thinking back to my first year of marriage and my first move. We were moving from college to seminary, and we had packed all of our belongings into the smallest U-Haul we could rent. We had no confirmed seminary registration, no jobs, no money, and no place to live. We did have a lot of faith that God would provide though; and, by the end of the first four days, we had been given all four of our necessities. "Could I still be that trusting?" I often wonder. I guess I want to believe I could, but I have to admit that I probably couldn't move ten miles today without a carefully selected pediatrician (one who has a twenty-four hour answering service) on call.

Of course, infant or no infant, moving to a new church is seldom a simple task; and it becomes increasingly more complicated if you also have to follow a good act. Picture, for example, this scene: Mrs. Personality has just removed her last crystal goblet from the parsonage kitchen. A large entourage of tearful church women help her out the door. "How can we ever get along," they moan, "without her original Christmas dramas—her fantastic church school lessons—her scrumptious cheese soufflés?" Waving a last rather sloppy good-bye, the mournful women turn back toward the parsonage driveway and run into . . . the new minister's wife, a soft-spoken introvert whose idea of a fun afternoon centers around sitting alone by a lake with a good book.

Fortunately, most transitions are much less abrupt; but even if some time has passed since the previous minister's wife prayed her final prayer (aloud and in public, no doubt), many women do find themselves starting new lives among people who remember every good deed their predecessors ever did. The result? Lots of ministers' wives end up spending their first weeks in a parsonage pounding their fists into plastic-covered chairs and groaning, "It's just too hard to be a minister's wife!" And it's true. It is hard to be a minister's wife. Believe me, I know. And yet, life is seldom a piece of cake, no matter whose wife you are. I also know that, and maybe that is why I get so excited whenever I meet a minister's wife who has developed the knack of seeing the joy in life too. Maybe that is why I believe it is so important for every minister's wife to work on developing that knack.

There's Something Funny about this Marriage

I really think that too much of the material written about ministers' wives is somber and heavy. I think there is too little emphasis on the crucial need for a sense of humor, on the simple ability to laugh, even at oneself. Sure, the ministry does have its serious overtones; but the longer I am involved in it, the more firmly I believe that much of it borders on the absolutely hysterical. I just can't get too serious, for example, about a man who holds up his over-sized King James and tells me that the least a minister's wife can do is read from the "real Bible"... or a woman who hints that it is my duty, as a minister's wife, to have another baby in order to increase Church School attendance. Every day, in fact, I am becoming more and more certain that the critical element in the life of the happy minister's wife is laughter—laughter which must begin, in my opinion, not too long after one's husband gets "The Call."

Moral:

The minister is the one who answers the call, but his wife is the one who needs directory assistance———.

2.
Toppling Pedestals

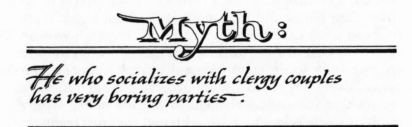

Myth:

He who socializes with clergy couples has very boring parties.

It is a well-known fact that every Christian family in the world has given up on the idea of long, formal, uninterrupted, daily family devotions—every Christian family, that is, except the minister's family. The minister's family is different. Those people still gather in front of the hearth every night promptly at 6:00 with their colorfully underlined Bibles and neatly typed prayer lists. Right? "No way," most of my peers exclaim. For, like it or not, ministers, too, live in a world of TV dinners and soccer meets and rush-hour kitchen traffic. They, too, have teen-aged sons who would rather clean their rooms than read the Bible with Mom and Dad. They have nine-year-old daughters who would stick their hands in the air and ask to go to the bathroom if anyone tried to read a Psalm to them.

If my family were ever on a pedestal, I am sure that it collapsed long ago; and I can't remember anyone mourning its passing. However, I do feel the need to ask a few troubling questions about the whole thing. Who, for example, builds the pedestals for ministers' families? Where did the perfection syndrome originate? And why am I supposed to be different from (better than) my next door neighbor, whose husband works for Kroger? It just doesn't make sense.

Peek-a-boo; I See You

For example, I seem to be expected to simply accept the fact that the ministry is a high visibility profession—and that my family, therefore, has been put on public display for life. Maybe this has something to do with the sense of awe that surrounds a clergyman (the assumption that a person who has God as his boss must have extremely interesting staff meetings), or maybe it has something to do with the idea that the ministry carries with it great power. And I suppose that an individual who can christen you, baptize you, marry you, bury you, and counsel you through each crisis in between does carry a little more clout than the paper boy.

And yet, the minister is not the only one who becomes highly visible as a result of his job. All of the people in his family are also singled out. They are assumed to be different, too, and they are watched rather closely. The unfortunate part of this is the fact that some people like to be watched much more than others do, and the women and children who didn't choose Daddy's profession in the first place are sometimes the ones who don't like it at all.

Of course, it is true that a minister's family is not

watched in the same way that a rock star walking into McDonald's would be watched. People never ask us for autographs or paper their walls with our pictures. They never faint at our feet. But we are watched in a fairly disconcerting way, for we are watched to see if we are going to step out of line.

The members of a minister's family are also watched to see if they are going to say the right things at the right times. For instance, I'll never forget the day my daughter asked me a simple question about one of her storybooks. "Yes, Becky," I said to my toddler, "Pinocchio's nose did grow whenever he told a lie," and I thought the discussion was over. How was I to know she would go around looking for people with long noses so that she could ask them if they tell lies? Granted, other children pull similar tricks, but a minister's child is "different"—which is probably why I still cringe whenever I think of what might have happened if my daughter had asked that question of the wrong long-nosed tither.

Plastic Parsonage People

Being on display is one thing, but lots of ministers' families are also protected from life in the real world. This doesn't happen to me too often, although I have walked in on a few jokes and unwittingly nipped them in the bud. ("Can you imagine the frustration of knowing 159 dirty jokes and no punch lines?" many clergy couples ask.) I have also been invited into a few homes with empty magazine stands. I don't know if people truly believe I've never seen a centerfold or if they want me to believe that they haven't. Either way though, the whole thing sounds like game playing; and I've never been particularly good at playing games.... "You're certainly welcome to attend our group meeting next Tuesday," I told a young woman who had just joined the church.

"Well, uh, uh, from what I've seen in the past, I just don't think I would fit in at a church women's meeting," she stammered.

"I know what you mean," I replied, "and I'm sure there are women's groups that live up to their questionable reputations." Then I went on to say, "In fact, I've even heard some people call them stitch-and-bitch societies." After my new friend did a double take to make sure she was still talking to the minister's wife, she began to laugh. And she was there the following Tuesday. Admittedly, my approach could have backfired, but I can't help but think that it doesn't really hurt anyone to find out that ministers' wives are human—which is, of course, the truth.

There are numbers of other ministers' wives who agree with me on this point. "I really believe that admitting we're imperfect makes people love us more," one of them explained, while another said that she thinks it is important for her to do everything possible to help people see her as a "fellow child of God, by no means perfect, but forgiven just like all other Christians."

Yes, the lady who dented our fender and expressed relief at having hit a minister instead of just a person really did have it all wrong. For, although the ministry does provide one with a unique way of serving God, the fact remains that my husband and I are nothing more than vessels available for God's use. And, along with the privilege of writing "Rev." before one's name does go the heavy responsibility of helping people understand that a minister is neither omniscient nor omnipresent.

"A young woman was shocked when I told her I sin," one minister's wife commented, and this is not an unusual story. Some people even talk themselves into believing that the minister's entire family is perfect—or at least that they should be. I would love to invite any such people to drop by my house and watch my daughter try to flush her stuffed lamb down the toilet, but I doubt that it would do any good. So, I guess I will just have to keep telling people that my family has no inside track with God, that God never has played favorites, and that ministers' families have emotional ups and downs just like everyone else.

It is true. Although it may be a well-kept secret, there are some days when ministers and their families don't even feel like going to church. Clergy couples seldom read the evening newspaper responsively either. And my husband and I make it a point never to use the words "thee" or "thou" when we are in bed together. Of course, in addition to experiencing all of the normal, healthy side effects of living the human life, a minister's family also has to struggle with hang-ups, anxieties, and sins—and lots of problems for which we have no magic answers.

And the Tension Mounts

Yes, in spite of all the self-help books, some ministers' wives do end up feeling very frustrated. Many of them end up feeling pretty bitter too. And when you add to that the great burden of guilt that is placed upon a wife who resents sharing her husband with God—or the fact that a husband who works for the supreme source of happiness and security and fulfillment is just not "allowed" to have a wife who is neither happy nor secure nor fulfilled—you can have a very volatile situation indeed.

There is no way of finding out how many ministers' wives are having serious trouble coping with their life-styles, and maybe it isn't important to know. Even if we did know how many there are, the reasons for their dissatisfaction would undoubtedly be as numerous and as varied as the women themselves. However, it is easy to see that there are quite a few ministers' wives in today's world who are speaking out about their negative feelings—and quite a few ministers' wives who admit that there is room for improvement in the parsonage life.

Take, for example, the minister's wife who talked about being in a church that provided no real support, financial or otherwise, for the minister and his family. "For me," she explained, "there have been some *very* difficult periods bordering on suicide and the need for periods of supportive, intensive counseling." She is certainly not the only minister's wife who has ever struggled through a bad church experience. Tragically though, many of the most unhappy ministers' wives feel that they have nowhere to go for help.

Does Your Parsonage Have a Trauma Center?

Who does counsel the counselor? What happens when a minister's family faces emotional dilemmas or family turmoil? Turn to a fellow pastor, and you would risk losing face among your surprisingly competitive peers. Go to your superiors, and you would fear that your next church might be situated on a fault line somewhere. Talk to someone in your congregation, and all hell would break loose for sure. By Sunday, Mrs. Big Mouth would know that your daughter is on the pill, and Mr. Moneybags would decide that you are forming a clique in the church because you told someone about it. Or so it seems.

The minister and his family carry a great burden when they have no one in whom to confide. And yet, many clergy families don't have anyone. They have no outlet, no place where they can struggle openly and share their troubles and receive the help they need to move forward and grow accordingly. As a result, many of them end up hiding their feelings, groaning to themselves, and then hurrying back to church for the next deacon's meeting (so that they can plan ways to minister to people who have problems). Lots of clergy families thus give the impression that they actually had it all together from the start, and most people do buy it. For, there are lots of ways to appear perfect if you never let anyone actually get to know you.

The Dead End Street Called Pretense

I tried to be perfect once for a while, but I couldn't pull it off. I always got the hiccups in the middle of the opening prayer or fell off the podium during the stewardship banquet. I never could even witness "right," and that used to bother me most of all. "Why can't I ever remember what comes after John 3:16?" I would rebuke myself, but it didn't help. People continued to get bored and wander off, and I continued to flip nervously through my Bible. Even today, it still bothers me to think how many lost souls might be roaming around right now because I couldn't find a tract in my cluttered tote bag.

Luckily, I did eventually learn some things about loving people into the Kingdom of God; and I no longer need to rely on my lousy memory to witness to them. I still have to contend with that lousy memory in other areas of my life though.... "I'm Mrs. Smith," the lady bubbled, "and I want you to know what a wonderful husband you have." Then she added, "I've only met him a few times, and he always remembers my name. Are you as good as your husband?"

"Well," I replied, ignoring the possible implications lurking inside her question, "I don't know, Mrs. er-a-Jones."

"You're not," she said dryly.

I survived that particular incident, but I still have dreams about being unable to remember the words to the "Doxology" and then being assigned permanent church nursery duty as punishment. Me? Perfect? What a laugh.

But lots of ministers' wives aren't laughing. For, while

the assumptions of perfection in the ministry and the truth about those assumptions may be miles apart, figuring out how to bridge the gap can be a very frustrating task. Sure, most of us know that our husbands are not going to lead anyone very far if they are afraid to admit that they need their congregations' love. We also know that we, ourselves, are going to do little more than stumble awkwardly through life if we are always wearing masks. And yet, we don't always project the kind of openness and honesty we really want to project.

I, for one, seemed to project the sweet, but scholarly, little angel image when I first became a minister's wife. I didn't really want to. It just sort of happened—and it quickly became a roadblock to my Christian growth process. For, in truth, I hardly knew who the apostle Paul was at that time. (When I was growing up, I was much more interested in learning how to apply lipstick than in learning how to sing the books of the Bible.) So, I fudged my way through the book of Acts for a long time before I developed enough nerve to tell anyone that I was one minister's wife who needed my fellow church members' help as much as they needed mine.

Moving beyond Pretend Play

Today I find it easier to be honest about my deficiencies and imperfections, and I think there are large numbers of ministers' wives in the world who could echo that statement. I think, too, that I finally understand what that wise pastor was saying when he prayed for my young, newly ordained husband, "I pray that you will be human," he said, "for you are called not only to minister, but to live a life of confession." Perhaps I'm a cockeyed idealist, but I really do believe that most people would rather build a relationship with a flesh-and-blood human being than with a clerical wind-up doll. I also believe that most ministers' wives would like to be those human beings—or, as many of them have told me, "just another lay person in the congregation." And I know, for sure, that I don't want people looking to me for absolute perfection, for I am bound, at some point, to let them down.

As a Christian, I have been taught that I must try to point people through me to Jesus Christ, the perfect model; but I am beginning to think that I may have to spend my life fighting against peoples' expectations in order to do it. Of course, I am not alone in my struggle. Even the wives of well-known ministers have to find ways to deal with the pedestal syndrome. Popular author/minister's wife Mrs. Charlie Shedd (Martha), for instance, explained that she handles her life in the public eye by thinking of herself simply as Charlie's wife, "the Charlie I have known since high school days."

I like her idea. In fact, if more people had known my own husband in high school, I am sure they would be much less likely to expect perfection from him today. After all, how much perfection could anyone expect from a person who went skinny-dipping with his brother in a forbidden creek—and even drove the getaway truck for a Halloween egg-throwing session. (Still, the skinny-dippers ended up with infected feet, and the Halloween mischief-makers made the mistake of throwing an egg at the town bully's car, so maybe a prospective minister *is* doomed to pay for his imperfections.)

At any rate, I really hate to think where I would be today if I had always pretended to be the perfect minister's wife. Once I even went through a time when I wasn't sure I believed in the organized church at all. This happened mostly because I was too tired of potluck dinners, and I simply needed the freedom and space to work that through. Had I been forced to ignore my feelings, however, I might be sitting home today writing hate mail to some pastoral relations committee just because of a few silly baked hams. Of course, there are times when a minister's wife needs more than freedom and space....

What's a Best Friend?

Sometimes a minister's wife needs people who care enough to risk getting involved, friends to talk with—not just "pretty-dress-you're-wearing-this-Sunday" friends, but "spilling-out-your-guts-when-needed" kinds of friends. Granted, a woman in any walk of life is lucky if she has a few of this kind of friend, but a minister's wife is probably extremely lucky if she has one.

"There is never a closeness to another woman, and there is a feeling of giving *all* the time," one minister's wife explained. "I feel used, and I want to share my feelings, but I don't because of possible ensuing gossip." And another minister's wife added that she once equated being in the church and having lots of people around with lack of loneliness. Instead, she found a lack of intimacy and a number of people who are afraid to get too close.

Why don't people want to get "too close" to their minister's family? Why are so many of us left sitting home watching Dick Clark every New Year's Eve? Why do we so often go alone to football games? Do people really believe that those long pastoral prayers are contagious? Or do they fear that a minister might get carried away and start preaching in the middle of a movie? Why don't people ever charcoal hamburgers with their ministers? (Church functions don't count.)

In Search of the Snag

I'm not sure anyone can actually trace the evolution of this curious behavior, although I suspect that, through the years, there have been just as many clergy couples who have welcomed prestige and power as there have been church people who have wanted to believe that ministers' families are superior in morality or holiness. Maybe it is just too easy to pretend; or maybe, as one minister's wife put it, "Some people need an example for their Christian walk while others need an excuse for their failure." Maybe. But that doesn't mean it is fair simply to say that we are all victims of circumstance and then leave it at that.

The other day I dug out the old tape of my husband's ordination ceremony. It was a good service, and it evidently "took"; but I couldn't believe the number of times the words "set apart" were used. Over and over the congregation was reminded that ordination means "different." Now, I have no real argument with the term "set apart." I know that a clergyman is ordained for an important work. I know that the ministry is special, and I believe that a servant of God should be respected as such. And yet, once a pastor begins his ministry, I think that the concept of "set apart" has to be very carefully defined.

... What a sense of awe I felt gazing up at that pulpit raised high above even my own daddy's head. I was eight years old, and I was listening to a big man in a long robe telling everyone how to live. I was thrilled. What power! What insight! I was in the presence of a spokesman of God himself. How appalled I would have been if anyone had suggested to me that my minister might enjoy playing hopscotch with me. No, I have nothing against ministers who step up into pulpits. The ones who never come down are the ones who bother me.

"Does a minister live in a church or in a home?" a small boy asked me one day.

"He lives in a home," I said, trying hard not to add, "at least part-time."

"Then he's sort of like me, isn't he?" the child replied.

Why doesn't anyone over the age of five ever ask me that kind of question? Why don't I ever hear such questions from any of those people who are on the verge of screaming hypocrisy and walking out of the church forever? Sure, I am glad to see growing numbers of ministers' wives' support groups and conferences springing up around the country, and I am glad to see denominational staffs and clergy boards working on ways to provide anonymous counseling services for their clergy families. But I would like to see more work being done in these areas. I would like to see more people taking these things more seriously. For, no matter how advantageous it may be for a clergyman to look perfect to the voting members of the "Pastor of the Year" award committee, pretense has never helped anyone reach out to people who are really hurting.

I have often asked classes of young people to list in order the individuals to whom they would go if they needed help. Ministers rarely make the charts, and they are never in the top ten. When asked why, the young people explain that they would rather go to peers who know nothing about counseling than go through the embarrassment of baring their souls to their pastors. "My pastor just wouldn't understand," they say. Little do they know. Not only would most pastors understand, but many of them have "been there." Admittedly though, there are some pastors who would rather give up their honorary doctorates than acknowledge that fact.

The Long Step Down

Ministering to people involves a very deep level of interpersonal relationship, and anyone who is detached from others can't possibly function effectively in a situation like that. That is why I believe it is so important for all clergy couples to look for ways to come down from their pedestals. That is why I believe it is essential for every clergy couple to realize how easy it is for ministers (or their wives) to find themselves in the position of being the last people left between a human being and the end zone of his destruction.

I have a minister friend who spent his longest night on a river with a young man who was lying on the barrel of a loaded shotgun. It was an old story. A girlfriend had chosen someone else. The minister finally talked the young man into giving life another chance, but he had to get dirty to do it. He had to crawl in the mud until he could convince a desperate human being that there would be no soap boxes, no pat answers. My minister friend had to overcome the temptation to appear perfect, and then he had to come all the way down from his pedestal—a difficult thing to do, no doubt. For the security and safety of the pedestal could have belonged to him for life, just for the asking, simply because he is a minister.

Moral :

Maybe some ministers can fool all of the people all of the time, but the minister who can fool his own wife is yet to be born.

3.

Back to Basic Black

Myth:

Definition of the perfect minister's wife—a woman who can peck out "Heavenly Sunlight" on the piano and who always leaves the parsonage door slightly ajar.

"They don't even have dress codes in high school anymore," I grumbled to my husband one day when I was browsing through a rack of rather skimpy swimwear. But my husband, who normally practices his listening skills on anyone but me, didn't hear me. He had already wandered off, and I was left alone to argue with myself. I'm still not sure who won my argument with myself that day, but I think my superego did. At any rate, I didn't buy any of those swimsuits. My choice, I decided, had more to do with the Christian model I am trying to give to the world than it did with my being a minister's wife... at least I think it did.

The Good Little Minister's Wife

The fact is that a number of people do expect their minister's wife to look a certain way. That certain way, although it is never actually spelled out, is probably best described as inexpensively presentable—sort of early sweetly dowdy, bargain basement style. Of course, no one ever seems to agree on the specific components of the "clergy look." Few people know, for example, whether or not the minister's wife can wear a bright red silk blouse. (She would certainly have to promise to leave only the top button unbuttoned.) And, some people aren't even sure whether or not she can wear slacks to church on Sunday nights. (Maybe it would be all right as long as 75 percent of the other church women have already been doing so for at least two and a half years.) It is almost enough to make one wonder if this unspoken dress code could be more a matter of a wife complementing, without upstaging, her minister husband (a man whose own wardrobe is supposed to include a pair of white patent leather shoes and several suits with that "master of ceremonies" look).

Even the way a minister's wife is expected to act is touched by ambiguity. For instance, she is supposed to be all things to all people; but she is also supposed to avoid friction at all costs. One Episcopal minister's wife put it this way: "The stereotype is one of being seen and not heard (sort of like what my grandmother used to say to me when I was five and talked too much at the dinner table)." I know what she means. I even know a few ministers' wives who refuse to visit friends in the hospital. "We might make someone mad because we can't visit everyone," they sigh, and I can sympathize with them. And yet, I can't help but think that a system that prevents women from visiting sick friends is a system in need of extensive overhaul.

Stereotypes also carry over into the area of conversation. "Shop talk" has reached epidemic proportions among some clergy couples, and I couldn't count the number of people who have waylaid me in the supermarket to explain why they didn't make it to church the preceding Sunday. "I never even asked!" I always exclaim to myself. "I wasn't thinking about church at all; I was thinking about the price of pot roast!" Generally, I walk away from that kind of encounter half convinced that I am incapable of discussing anything that doesn't take up an offering.

Many people expect a minister's wife to be a great cook too—not the elaborate ingredients and lavish dishes kind of cook, but the kind of cook who can turn out pure country gourmet on a shoestring. For, every minister's wife is just supposed to have the inborn potential to turn out flawless turkey dinners with kitchen equipment that some church member junked by way of the parsonage. I try to tell people how silly this is. "My pet fantasy is the dream of someday finding a house that doesn't even have a kitchen," I explain. No one really believes me though. So I continue to search for the ultimate package dinner, and everyone else continues to believe that somewhere inside me there is a miniature Betty Crocker just waiting for her big chance to come out and dust off the crumbs.

"Winning" by Default

Ministers' wives who feel bound by any or all of the preceding stereotypes often accept their lots in life like martyrs. They abide by the dictated styles of attitude, action, and dress; and they tell themselves that living out the stereotype to perfection is their only hope of finding true happiness. As a result, instead of yearning to break out of their molds, they yearn to bake the perfect covered dish. And that is where the real danger lies. Not only are such women perpetuating the idea that ministers' wives do conform to a distinct pattern, but the pattern itself is someone else's pattern.

"I resent it," a minister's wife from a small town explained when asked about stereotypes. "It discourages me, and I often, inwardly and invisibly, throw up my hands and just bow out of the picture." This woman went on to say that she tries to cope with this by putting energy into community work, but she said she would rather be working as hard directly on behalf of the church. Another minister's wife added that one of her peers used to do a perfect job of performing. "She was all sweetness and light," the woman said, "until she had a breakdown."

Still, many of us do go the stereotype route, at least for a while. I certainly did, although my "best little hostess this side of heaven" period was an extremely short one. My fresh-perked coffee was always so terrible that everyone asked me to go back to instant, and my foolproof pecan pie usually came out of the oven with the crust in the center. ("How quaint," a charter church member once cringed.) If I had really been cut out to be a wonderful hostess, things might have turned out differently. As it was, I shudder to think of the self-image I would have cultivated had I spent my life searching for fulfillment in the perfect quiche.

I don't really think that anyone misses my hostess period, and few of the people in my church seem to be overly interested in my wardrobe or my culinary expertise. Maybe their attitudes are not so unusual after all. And yet, some ministers' wives do feel that old stereotypes abound in certain areas of the country—and that denomination and type of church also make a difference. Take, for instance, the minister's wife from a small rural church who said that she and her husband used to have a lot "Waltonian ideas about small town life." When her expectations were not realized, when the members of her particular congregation would not relinquish their preconceived notions about the ministry, she ended up feeling very disillusioned.

Of course, many ministers' wives hasten to add that things used to be worse. Like the North Carolina minister's wife of twenty-nine years who said she used to hide her real self more in the early years of her husband's ministry. "Social customs seemed to dictate it then," she explained. Some ministers' wives contend that much of the pressure forced upon them comes from husbands or from one or two individuals. Such pressure, they believe, can and should be directly confronted. Perhaps they are right. And yet, for one reason or another, numbers of today's ministers' wives do continue to feel some pressure from their churches.

Inside the Fishbowl

Strangely enough, one of the places where many ministers' wives feel pressured is in the "privacy" of their own homes. "We live in Grand Central Station," they sigh, "and the train never arrives." At least a part of this dilemma is usually blamed on the tradition of church-owned parsonages. And it is true that almost everyone who lives in "someone else's home" is more than eager to provide detailed descriptions of lousy plumbing, leaky roofs, and chipped paint. Occasionally, such people even have a few horror stories to tell.

Take, for example, the minister's wife who talked about arriving home to find people lounging around her living room and rummaging through her refrigerator. She said that locks on the parsonage doors were considered no-noes for her family and that the trustees even wanted to examine their income tax reports one year. "I resorted to swearing under my breath after not doing such a thing since my conversion in 1957," she groaned.

Conversely, clergy couples who own their own homes seldom talk about clogged drains. Instead, they talk about the joys of retirement with equity. They talk about how great it is to forget that anyone who moves Mr. Tuttle's

generously donated musical bookcase does so only under
threat of eviction—and how refreshing it is to stop hiding
the kids' marking pencils (in order to keep the "church's"
walls spotless). Large numbers of ministers' wives, then,
do seem to favor home ownership. "The possibility of a
woman being thrown out of her home in the event of her
husband's illness or death is just not a very cheery thought
to write home to Mother about," they explain, and they
certainly do have a point. Especially if Mother has never
really gotten over her daughter marrying the minister instead of that nice young premed student.

There is another side to this issue though, for it is becoming increasingly difficult for anyone to own a home in
this age of soaring housing costs. Some of today's
churches are facing this dilemma and finding ways to
solve it—by forming housing committees to work out new
kinds of clergy living arrangements or by offering housing
retirement funds or financial plans through which a pastor
can share in parsonage appreciation. Hopefully, this trend
will continue to grow. And yet, it must be said that nothing, not even home ownership, can offer the members of a
minister's family an absolute guarantee that they will
never feel the effects of fishbowl living. Sometimes the
fishbowl feeling simply seems to "be there" no matter
what.

A Fishbowl Title Search

Could it be that clergy families themselves are a part of
the problem? Could it be that our reluctance to tell people
how we really feel has set the scene for all those after-
hours telephone inquiries about next month's church
bowling party? I'm not sure, but I think it may be possible.
And I do believe that many of the people who try to dump
the fishbowl on the minister do so unintentionally.
Perhaps much of it is even a result of innocent and mis-

directed enthusiasm that could easily be re-channeled. I guess I believe this partly because I, myself, have been caught on both sides of the trap.

I will never forget the experience of being a pre-teen and having a crush on my pastor. (No, I was not nursing a subconscious desire to marry a minister; I also had a crush on two student teachers and one meter reader at the same time.) The pastor in question was unfortunate enough to live in a home that adjoined the church, and I was always in it—dusting. I honestly thought I was helping the minister's wife, and my parents were probably just glad I was being kept out of trouble. Evidently, no one thought about guiding me toward a more proper path and dusting me out the door. Had they done so in a gentle way, I am sure I would have gone home cheerfully. As it was, I seldom went home at all. Forgive me, Reverend, wherever you are.

Today people tend to guard their privacy with their lives, and I can't imagine too many of them not understanding that the minister's family needs some too—which may be as good a reason as any for a minister's wife to be honest about her feelings. Of course, it should be said that the parsonage revolving-door concept bothers some ministers' wives much more than it bothers others. Such differences in attitude could probably be traced back to the way each minister's wife was raised. I, for example, was raised by a kind-hearted father who worked as a toll collector on a bridge.

Yes, my dad's idea of a successful evening centered around meeting a drifter who couldn't afford the toll and bringing the fellow home with him. My mother, on the other hand, did not share my dad's enthusiasm about surprise visitors. In fact, she usually threw several fits before she calmed down enough to make sandwiches for everyone. I ended up somewhere in between, but I did come out of that home with the ability to see both sides fairly clearly.

To Sink, or to Swim

Each minister's wife is an individual human being, a woman with a unique background and a unique personality. Each minister's wife, therefore, is bound to feel and act differently inside her individual home. Some ministers' wives, for instance, live by the motto, "Yes, you are welcome in my home, but...."; and they insist on making that fact clear to everyone. Others keep the coffeepot on simmer and hope for at least one unexpected guest a day. As long as everyone is happy, who is to say some are right and the others wrong? The ones who pour the coffee while they, themselves, remain on "simmer" are the only ones who worry me.

All of this, then, is yet another endorsement of the need for each minister's wife to understand herself and to put that understanding into practice. But this isn't always an easy thing to do. I know some ministers' wives, for example, who feel that they have to be properly dressed and ready to receive guests twenty-four hours a day. Not because they enjoy living like that, but because they are afraid to change. Occasionally, when I am puttering around my own house, I think of those women and wonder if they will ever know how much pure joy can be found in a pair of grimy cut-offs and a faded T-shirt—and I feel very concerned for the people who persist in letting old stereotypes clutter up their lives.

The Birth of the Stereotype

I'm not sure that anyone knows where any of the minister's wife stereotypes actually originated. My guess is that some of them could be traced clear back to the monastic practice of emphasizing Christian commitment by withdrawing from and renouncing the world and the things of it. Some traditions might also have been passed down to us from the Puritan era, while others could have been derived from the strict codes of behavior and rules of etiquette that are a part of the history of our country. And yet, I can't help but think how awful it would be if we someday found out that all of those old stereotypes were dreamed up by a little group of ministers' wives who wanted to get back at God for keeping their husbands from going to Law School or something. . . .

Oh well. I suppose we'll never know the full truth, and it probably doesn't do much good to search for people to blame for unfortunate circumstances anyway. Besides, stereotypes have probably always varied from place to place, church to church, and era to era. The real issue, then, must be the fact that somewhere on the other side of it all, we ended up with that nice little minister's wife who should be seen and not heard. And, although I'm not really sure exactly how we did this, I recently ran across a book that helped me understand a little bit about the ways some of my predecessors in the parsonage tried to cope with their roles in life. The book, entitled *Quiet Hints to Ministers' Wives*, was written in 1934.

"We women of the parsonage would be wondrously wise if we said little or nothing about our own troubles," the author wrote. "What can a husband do with a dyspeptic and complaining wife?" Then she continued this line of thought by talking about the need to cast one's burden upon God instead of upon one's husband, for . . . "Joy and rest come to the hustling, careworn minister when he finds his mistress of the manse gladhearted, and radiating cheer, smiles and sunshine."[1]

Advice like this, although it is very different from what we are now taught about psychological and marital well-being, may have worked in the thirties. I don't know. But

---

1. Frances Sandys Elson, *Quiet Hints to Ministers' Wives* (Boston: The Stratford Company Publishers, 1934), p. 7.

it doesn't seem to work too well in today's world, and maybe that is the real issue. Maybe too many ministers' wives have never updated any of it to fit into their contemporary, individual situations.

Toward a Wardrobe of Many Colors

So where do we go from here? How do we make peace with our long history of written and unwritten rules? How do we separate the good from the bad, and how do we unload those customs that prevent us from being ourselves? I really believe that the first step has to involve a conscious, daily effort to separate bias from gospel, at least until each minister's wife has discovered for herself the person that God created her to be. For, in the midst of our searches, some of us may even find out that we really do like to wear black all the time or, heaven forbid, that we love to lead junior high choirs. We may discover that we would do these things even if we were married to movie producers. In that case, of course, those choices would be the right ones because they would be our own.

I, on the other hand, know that I would never make it as a minister's wife if low-heeled pumps and "Heavenly Sunlight" were prerequisites for me. That is why I need some specific, concrete ways to cope with the stereotypes that pop up around me. Lots of other ministers' wives express this same need, too; and many of them seem to be finding solutions that work well for them. There are some ministers' wives, for instance, who attempt to tease people out of putting them into boxes. Other ministers' wives try to strike a balance between living up to people's expectations and living according to one's own convictions. Then, there are those ministers' wives who simply ignore the stereotypes, choosing instead to verbalize their intentions to be themselves.

Of course, no matter what direction one chooses, few

people seem to believe that success can be achieved overnight. Mrs. Louis Evans, Jr. (Colleen Townsend Evans), in fact, warns that it often takes some time for individuals to accept ministers' wives as real people. "Not all do," explained the wife of the pastor of the National Presbyterian Church in Washington, D.C., "but God gives us the inner security to live with the fact that we disappoint some people."

It is true. Whatever we do, we are bound to disappoint some people. That is why the desire to keep peace at all costs is not a very good excuse for ending up as the hardest working off-key soprano in the church choir—just as the desire to be liked by everyone is not a very good reason for pretending to be the impeccable minister's wife in that dusty old novel (instead of the minister's wife who skipped out of Wednesday night prayer meeting to read it). Granted, we may have to live with the fallout from old stereotypes for some time to come; but that doesn't mean that we have to fade into the woodwork. It doesn't mean we have to stop trying. In fact, there are large numbers of ministers' wives who are lovingly and prayerfully claiming their rights to be themselves every day; and I have never heard of one of them being thrown out of the church on the grounds of irreconcilable skirt lengths.

Set Free to Soar

In essence, the truth is probably summed up in the old story of the village factory owner who always set his clock by the clock in the jewelry shop window—while the jeweler set his clock by the factory whistle. Most of us know that we need to measure ourselves, not against people's expectations, but against those of Jesus Christ. We know that we need to make choices according to what we perceive as God's plan for us, not according to the quirks of the chairman of some church board. We also know that the minister's wife who is honest enough to rip through all the veneer is the one who eventually gets the glimpse of the human being God originally thought up when he made her. And yet, many ministers' wives still find it hard to live life as though it were a joy instead of a burden. Many ministers' wives find it hard to clean out all of the junk that gets in the way.

A couple of weeks ago I was stumbling through my house trying to prove that I could put away the dinner dishes, dry a load of clothes, wash my hair, and perform minor surgery on a drink-and-wet doll, all in simultaneous rhythm. Much to my chagrin, I ended up looking nothing like a Superwoman and very much like a junior high role play of the story of Mary and Martha. "Enough!" I yelled.

"What's wrong, Mommy?" my daughter asked softly.

"What do you mean what's wrong?" I erupted. "I have ten million things to do! That's what's wrong, and I have to be ready to go to the Bible study in twenty minutes!"

"Then why're you going to church tonight?" she replied.

"Because your daddy's the minnnn... ," I almost blurted out, but I caught myself in time. "Why do you think I'm going, Becky?" I said, trying to match my child's calm tone.

"Cause you love Jesus," she replied, and then she casually returned to her menagerie of stuffed pets.

That is when I suddenly realized that my daughter was, in fact, correct. At the same time though, I also realized that her statement might not have been correct a few years ago. Back then, loving Jesus might only have been my number two reason for going. Today, however, I actually believe that my rationale has very little to do with my image. And, if I've been able to reveal the real me to one person (a ridiculously truthful, painfully perceptive three-year-old is no snap, believe me), then maybe the rest of the world can't be far behind after all.

Moral :

Most ministers' wives shouldn't live-in fishbowls (especially if they have lousy backstrokes and are married to men who haven't completed their CPR training).

4.
Warming the Bench

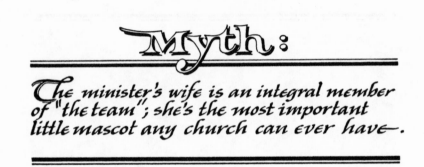

The minister's wife is an integral member of "the team"; she's the most important little mascot any church can ever have.

One summer, when I was teaching sixth graders in Bible School, the members of my class decided to formulate some questions they would like to ask God. An especially enthusiastic youngster (who fully expected God to drop by for an interview within the week) jotted down the question, "What is your job description, God?" We discussed the possibilities for a long time, and the children were very attentive. My own mind, however, was nowhere near the heavenly realm that day. Instead, I kept thinking about the fact that I had never really developed a job description of my own for my life in the church.

Lots of ministers' wives have trouble defining their specific roles in the church. Maybe that is why it is so easy to fall into the trap of trying to fill the shoes of the previous minister's wife, even if those shoes don't fit. Most likely, the previous minister's wife did the same thing with the shoes of the one before her too. And, although such women probably ended up turning into pumpkins much more often than they ended up wearing glass slippers, that practice has undoubtedly continued through the years. Still today, in fact, it is commonly used to establish the "place" of the minister's wife in the church—a place which, as a result, is often situated in the choir loft, the toddler room, or the kitchen. Not that there is anything wrong with a minister's wife being in any of those places if she so chooses; but it is certainly possible to carry the "minister's wife behind the teapot" role to extremes, just as it is possible for a church to end up with a minister's wife who is an ex officio member of everything and a real member of nothing.

Am I My Husband's Keeper?

Too many ministers' wives know exactly what it feels like to be automatically disqualified for responsible jobs in the church. One such woman, who expressed strong feelings about this, contends that this is a condition of our fallen state. She is not alone. Numbers of ministers' wives can recall times when they have felt compelled to act invisible in front of church nominating committees—or to remain neutral when certain church issues were being discussed. Sometimes this sort of thing even happens often enough to cause a minister's wife to feel as if her entire mind and body have been placed in neutral.

Lots of ministers' wives also resent being thought of as female clones of their minister husbands. "I'm never recognized unless I'm in the company of my husband," numbers of them insist, "and I got higher grades than he

did in graduate school!" Some even say they have thought
about installing telephone message centers in their homes
and then retiring into oblivion. "At the sound of the
tone," the voice would say, "please leave your name, a
short description of your problem, and a statement of your
willingness to serve on future church boards."

I, myself, spent quite a bit of time observing all kinds of
ministers' wives in all kinds of roles before I mustered up
enough courage to start carving out my own niche in the
church. Consequently, I found out that you have to know
yourself pretty well before you can even begin to do this.
How many introverts, for example, spend their lives leading the choir just because they never accept the fact that
they are behind-the-scenes people? Or what about the
minister's wife who plunges into the role of unsalaried
assistant pastor simply because she is not in touch with
her ambition to run for a seat on the school board?

Let There Be Options

There are lots of ways to help and support a husband,
even a husband who is a minister. The key to success,
however, is found in matching those ways to one's own
abilities and interests and gifts. At least that's what the
satisfied ministers' wives are saying. A Church of God
minister's wife, for example, feels that God truly prepared
her to be a minister's wife. She said that she began her
marriage wanting to be a joint partner in her husband's
ministry and that this role has worked well for her. Today
she believes that she complements her husband's ministry
in a special way because her personality is different from
his and because she can meet people "on a different
plane."

Other ministers' wives throw up red flags at anything
that even faintly resembles piggybacking on the successes
and failures of their husbands' ministries. These women

talk about how necessary it is for a minister's wife to have lots of outside interests; and they stress the importance of letting pulpit committees know that you get "two for one" only at a discount store, never at a church. I can certainly understand such feelings because I was once caught in the "two for one" snare myself. It happened back when my young student husband was still attempting to identify his gifts in the ministry.

"You want to try leading a student revival?" I groaned. "You've got to be kidding. It's bad enough to get drafted, but you want to volunteer for torture!" My logic was wasted on my young spouse though. He went right ahead and volunteered to try his hand at preaching—and I was the one who got drafted. Of course, I couldn't really blame him. Neither of us knew that the speaker's wife would be expected to play the piano for the entire week; and, when we finally found out, it was too late to refuse. So I gave it a try, managing, in the process, to make two of the church's already terrible anthems sound even more terrible. Then I bowed out. And my husband, probably not coincidentally, soon enrolled in the School of Religious Education.

Spring Training

Fortunately, many of today's ministers' wives have already discovered that the role of catchall pianist is not the only role in the church. Take, for instance, the woman who wants to support her husband's ministry but doesn't want to be a starting player on the team. Maybe she is one of those women who has gotten stuck carrying the ball single-handedly often enough to know what it feels like to be tackled by the whole team. Maybe not. At any rate, she can simply choose to stay on the sidelines and keep her ears and eyes open to people's needs and concerns—or she can find other ways to serve without always being in center stage. And, many of the ministers' wives who do this sort of thing are quick to explain that they feel it is very good for the church. A Michigan-based minister's wife, for example, views her role as one of "building up the brethren." She defined this as "phasing myself out as others take over," and she leads a very happy and fulfilled life.

Tom McGloshen, a professional counselor who has had experience working with ministers and their wives in developing personal and career goals, put it this way, "We find all sorts of variations—from the woman who wanted to marry a minister, but is unhappy with her lot to the woman who had never pictured herself in a manse, but is finding a great deal of satisfaction there." Then he went on to add, "Whether or not ministers' wives are prepared for their roles is more a function of the personality make-up of the individual than of the profession."

Thus, each minister's wife must select a path and make it distinctively her own, and different ministers' wives will undoubtedly make different selections. Most ministers' wives, however, do seem to agree on certain aspects of their roles. For instance, large numbers of them say they want their roles in the church to be those of lay people. They say they want to be viewed as fellow workers, as ministers only in the sense that all Christians are ministers, never as second-banana pastors. In order to be viewed this way, though, a minister's wife does have to be willing to let go and try her own wings; and this is not always an easy thing to do.

"Becky," I pleaded with my screaming child, "I know you have a cold and your nose is stuffy, but the reason you can't breathe well enough to sleep is because you're sucking your thumb." She looked at me dubiously. "If you will remove the thumb, you'll be able to breathe through your mouth," I continued. She looked at her thumb dubiously. Then, after a long pause, she plopped the prized digit back into her mouth and gave me one of those "leave me alone" looks. No matter how much misery she would have to endure, she wasn't about to give up the security of that thumb.

On the surface, this seemed ridiculous to me, not at all worthy of such an intelligent child. Then it dawned on me. I know a lot of ministers' wives who are just like that; and, what's more, I used to be one of them. I never sucked my thumb, but I clung so tightly to the security of my husband's "robetails" that I couldn't breathe either. As a result, I almost ended up resigning myself to a whole lifetime of holding on, a life built around the Charlie Brown philosophy of only dreading one day at a time.

Beyond Dirty Diapers and Bible Charades

Maybe I could always sense that ministers' wives who choose to create their own special roles in the church have to face some very real obstacles along the way. Or maybe I was just a slow learner. I don't know. I do know, however, that it took me quite a while to act on my need to be me. And I know that it took me even longer to learn how to spot the traps that have snared many a minister's wife. Take the "interests outside the church" approach for example. There are some ministers' wives who fall into the trap of living their entire lives outside the church merely because they never come to grips with the fact that they resent their husbands' roles inside it. That is probably why so many people warn against a minister and his wife going in opposite directions too often. "Sure you marry the man, not the profession," a minister's wife from New Jersey stated. "It is only later that you come to realize that the two are inseparable."

Step #1: Communicating

Discussing one's role with one's husband is probably an essential key. For, in the words of Mrs. David Mains (Karen), author of *Open Heart, Open Home,* "Many men take positions without a thought as to whether or not their wives will fit." Then she added, "David wouldn't accept a call to a ministry situation where my gifts would be unacceptable to the congregation."

Women who choose to live their entire lives inside the church have to contend with other kinds of traps. Like the minister's wife who chooses to volunteer for every job in the parish simply because she has no life outside it. She could very well wind up being one of those women who spend their lives clipping microphones onto their husbands' lapels and pushing their spouses out into center stage, the kind of minister's wife who sits in the wings and lives life vicariously. Such a woman usually ends up getting someone else's "strokes" secondhand—and then discovering that this is never good enough.

I have a friend who believes that a person needs seven hugs a day in order to be successful in business and at least four just to be psychologically normal. If this is even partially true, some of us are in deep trouble. That is why I have decided that all ministers' wives who look for success only inside their husbands' achievements should practice screaming, "Yes, you're right; the minister looks handsome in his three-piece-suit, but that's only because I pressed it!" Expression and communication of one's true feelings—the crucial key once again.

Communication becomes even more important when the element of competition begins to creep into the picture. In the words of Mrs. Richard Halverson (Doris), wife of the well-known clergyman/author, "Often women take on such a dominant role in the church that they usurp their husbands' leadership. What couples do to each other is a very subtle thing. Many have to live a long time to realize the deep hurt caused by confusion of roles, so one needs to be as aware as possible of how the role she chooses affects her partner."

Still, it is easy for me to say that a minister's wife should get in touch with her feelings and create her own role in the church; but it is much more difficult for me to do this—every day—in the knowledge that I grow and change and often act inconsistently and unpredictably. In fact, I even have trouble trying to explain my choices to other people; and I am not the only one. For, no matter how gently any minister's wife does this, there always seem to be some people who have trouble understanding her role, others who disagree with it, and still others who respond by patting her on the head and humoring her. Perhaps this is why so many of us end up inserting a few compromises into our original plans.

Step #2: Compromising

One of the most popular compromises is the "prayer in public" compromise. The minister's wife agrees to sign on the dotted line under "I hereby promise to provide opening prayers for any and all church functions until the year 2010" in return for certain concessions. Many ministers' wives believe that this is a small price to pay for not having to lead the rhythm band in the kindergarten room. And yet, even a trade-off like this is still a definite compromise, particularly for those women who don't find it easy to pray before large groups—or to whip out prayer number 430 on demand.

An Ohio minister's wife, for example, said that she manages to accept her compromise only by reminding herself that the day will come when she can make up for lost time. She explained it like this: "I don't know why the minister's wife is always asked to give the invocation at everything. The doctor's wife is not asked to sew up wounds. The dentist's wife never cleans teeth. They always announce it at the last minute too, so you don't dare say no. I've been doing it for thirty-one years now, and one of the reasons I'm looking forward to retirement is to have fun saying no (sweetly, of course)" ... which brings up yet another difficult task faced by each minister's wife who is trying to be herself. The task of learning how to say no, sweetly, of course.

Step #3: Learning When to Say No

"How do we refuse to work in programs that our own husbands developed?" the minister's wife asks. "And how do we say no to committees made up of people who pay our husbands' salaries?" Clearly, there is nothing simple about practicing the fine art of saying no; but, at the same time, I suspect that the complexity of it is often heightened by the minister's wife herself. At least it has been so for me, and I think I have finally figured out why. I believe it goes back to the time when I first began asking people to take responsibilities in the church—and listening to a string of responses that would easily qualify for *Ripley's Believe It or Not*.

"No, honey, I'd better not. My mother led the youth group back in 1904, and her arthritis got worse every year after that." Or, "I'd really love to serve on the Board of Trustees, but two years ago I developed a chronic allergy to stress." Then there is the classic, "I went to Sunday School when I was a kid, and I learned everything I need to know back then." I'm sure I could catalogue at least two hundred excuses for lack of Sunday School involvement alone. At one time, I even used to think up all sorts of sarcastic responses for them. "What, Mrs. Smith? You're willing to risk saying no to God, and you don't even have a lightning rod on your home?" Eventually though, I began to sublimate my desire for revenge into the acceptable channel. I started working off my excess energy by doing all of the jobs myself.

Before long, I noticed that the word "no" had pretty much disappeared from my own church vocabulary. I also noticed that I was doing too many things ever to be able to do any of them very well. I had thus fallen into yet another trap, the trap of spending too much time at church. Soon, I was volunteering for jobs for which I had no qualifications whatsoever. One year I even joined the church garden club, and I break out in hives every time I get near a hoe. Then there was the time when I agreed to teach the Ten Commandments to a bunch of rowdy third graders, knowing full well that I am barely capable of disciplining a "Pet Rock." That particular experience took place several years ago, but some of those students still think that the ninth commandment is "Thou shalt not lie down and bear false witness."

Still, it took me a long time to understand the difference between saying no to God and saying, "No, but... I am willing to use my talents in this other job" to people. I understand the concept now though, and I can toss out my negatives with a reasonable amount of polish these days. Sometimes I can even say no when I'm being recruited by the minister himself—unless he walks through the door with a dozen roses and a better idea, that is, for I've never been able to turn down a good bribe.

Step #4: Learning When to Say Yes

When I finally began to enjoy my chosen role in the church, I thought I had it made at last. Little did I know. Now I have to struggle even harder with the problem of figuring out how to put that role into practice; and I know I am not alone in my struggle. "Can I ask why $200,000 has been tied up in a flower fund for thirty years, or would I be placed on probation for asking such a radical question?" some ministers' wives wonder. "Should I explain why I feel that 'Tracing the History of Stainless Tableware' is an inappropriate program for a church reach-out group?" others ask. As usual, there are no easy answers.

There are some ministers' wives (the ones who are convinced that people in attendance at any meeting called for the purpose of discussing church business have already left their rational selves outside the sacred walls) who decide that it is best to keep their mouths shut. Others, however, decide to go ahead and speak out in a spirit of reconciliation and then let the eyebrows fall where they may. Sometimes the "sock it to them in love" approach works well, and the church people end up looking like they have just stepped out of a tranquil scene from *Camelot*. Other times, the whole thing ends up looking more like a fight scene from *The Dirty Dozen*.

Of course, the fear of making someone angry is not always the reason behind a minister's wife's hesitation to follow her chosen path in the church. Some ministers' wives just feel too inadequate to do what they really want to do, and I can understand such feelings. For, it probably wouldn't hurt any of us to have a little extra training in counseling technique or to take advantage of more of the continuing education opportunities around us. Also involved in all of this, however, may be the fear of being unfairly typecast.

Sure, the minister's wife knows that women's roles in all areas of society have changed. She also knows that her desire to assert her chosen lifestyle in her church is not the kind of desire that would ever result in the attempt to incite violent revolts among her people. She may even be a woman who wouldn't know how to stage a sit-in in an easy chair. And yet, many ministers' wives are running scared—terrified that a personal display of independent thinking would be dreadfully misinterpreted.

Preaching Really Is Easier than Practicing

How important it is for a minister and his wife to nurture each other in the role discovery process. How important it is for them to understand and support each other's roles. Take, for example, the minister's wife who really likes to tag along on home visits. Her husband needs to know this, because some women would rather pull church K.P. duty than make a pastoral call. (By the way, if anyone is looking for visitation guidelines, I, personally, accompany my husband only if he is going to pay a call on a high-fashion model.)

Of course, even with ample support from one's spouse, it still takes a lot of courage for a minister's wife to make her own decisions, communicate those decisions in love, and stand behind them in the patient hope that most people will eventually accept her as she is. One minister's wife who feels strongly about the importance of being oneself no matter what explained this by saying that she and her husband always find the same kinds of people in every church. "This is both good and bad," she added. "For, in each church, there are people who support us and those who don't."

Many other ministers' wives talked about how important it is to be patient with oneself. Mrs. Billy Graham (Ruth), for example, believes that a minister's wife, particularly a young one with children, really shouldn't feel compelled to do everything in the church. "After the children are grown," Ruth Graham explained, "if she has the gift or feels so led, there will be plenty of time to teach a Bible class or a Sunday School class."

Numbers of ministers' wives probably do overextend themselves in their churches, at least on occasion, and sometimes even to the point where it keeps them from spending quality time with their families. "Who wants to go home to hot dogs and dust balls again?" such women may ask themselves, and they are, thus, tempted just to give up and join another committee. Often, during such times, the minister's wife is neither understanding enough nor patient enough with herself. But why? Why would a minister's wife ever get herself into such a mess?

Why, Indeed?

I have asked myself that question many times, and I have finally concluded that I often invite trouble by allowing my faith to get too flabby. Faith. It is always the critical element behind a Christian's sense of patience. And faith certainly doesn't come into a person's life simply because he has the words "Rev. and Mrs." printed on his return address labels. Rather, a Christian, even a minister's wife, has to practice believing that God can use her in the situation in which she finds herself. She has to practice believing that God is working in her daily life, and she has to practice hoping against hope that he is working in the lives of the "impossible" people around her too.

I know one minister who thinks that the waters of the Red Sea didn't begin to part until Moses had taken the first step into them. This clergyman backs up his idea with his understanding of the Hebrew words in the Exodus account. I don't know if he is right or wrong, but I do know that there have been times when I have been afraid to get my own feet wet... and those times usually turned out to be the stumbling blocks that precluded me from being the person I really wanted to be. "If only I had known," I always told myself afterward, when I should have been saying, "If only I had exercised my faith in God."

Off the Bench at Last

Obviously, the whole task of developing one's role in the church involves a never-ending process of communication—communication with God, communication with one's husband, and communication with oneself. Like most ministers' wives, I try very hard to keep all the communication channels open; but, also like most minister's wives, my efforts are not always successful. I remember one time, for example, when I didn't communicate with anyone....

My husband was about to begin his ministry in a new church, and I just knew I would be asked to preside over many different kinds of women's meetings there. So, I decided to be a good little minister's wife (my first mistake) and do my homework ahead of time. As a result, I arrived at my new home dragging along a turquoise file box stuffed with stacks of original women's programs. We spent six years at that church, and I was never once asked to address a women's group. For a long time afterward, I couldn't figure out why. Then one day I mentioned it to my husband. "Why doesn't anyone ever take advantage of my fabulous expertise?" I moaned.

"I always do," he said.

"Not that kind of expertise, silly! I mean all those women's programs I wrote!"

"Well," he replied, "how many people actually know you have that turquoise file box?"

Moral:

A minister's wife must always be prepared to back up her turquoise file box with an effective (but loving) advertising campaign.

5.

But What Does He Do
for a Living?

Myth:

Find a minister's wife who works outside her home, and you've found a minister's wife whose church hasn't met its budget for three consecutive years.

On a rainy afternoon not long ago I was sitting at the desk in the den (which is also the sewing room, guest room, hobby room, and family room) trying to figure out what to do with the $3.52 left in the checking account. I couldn't decide whether to blow it on a week's supply of sugarless gum or buy a teaspoonful of gasoline and drive to the corner grocery to window shop. Before I could make the big choice I was interrupted by my noisy, but lovable, daughter and her five-year-old friend. They were pushing doll carriages through the house and talking about their families.

"What does your daddy do for a living?" the five-year-old asked.

"I think he's a preacher," my daughter replied.

"But what does he do for a living?"

I am always amazed at how much wisdom can acciden-
tally fall from the lips of a person who hasn't even started
kindergarten yet. "Perceptive kid," I mused to myself.
About that time the preacher, himself, peeked around the
door and flashed me one of those broad, ministerial smiles
(the kind that is a prerequisite for admission to any seminary). He announced that he should be congratulated for
remembering that I had a birthday coming up, and he
asked me what kind of gift I wanted. "Anything with a
designer label will do," I said dryly and promptly forgot
the whole conversation.

When my birthday arrived, I got some Pierre Cardin
soap. I was more than satisfied. It was certainly better than
I could have done on $3.52. And yet, I can't honestly say
that I've never fantasized about being married to a man
who could actually have afforded the dress. Of course,
fantasies have little to do with real life; and, on a rational
level, I do know that it is better to be married to a man I
love than to have all the trimmings. Besides, at the risk of
sounding too much like a minister's wife, I don't think I
ever really wanted to have a whole lot of money anyway.

They Called It "Easy Street"

When I was growing up my dad used to talk about how
miserable rich people are. He sort of convinced me; but I
don't think he ever convinced my mother, for she would
always make some cryptic statement about wishing she
could just have enough money to feel comfortable. It
bothered her more than she admitted, I suspect, because
when I (her only child) married a penniless student, she
asked me if retirement homes for paupers are comfortable.

I have never figured out exactly what being comfortable
entails, although I imagine it would take a lot more money
to get there today than in my mother's day. I know, at

least, that any child on my block would declare bankruptcy in a minute if he didn't have, at the absolute minimum, a ten-speed bike and a season pass to the nearest amusement park. And what mother wants her first-born son to be the only kid in the fifth grade without a good set of headphones and a pair of Adidas shoes?

So, the search for comfort continues in our world today; and, in the midst of this kind of world, we must live and love and build friendships and rear children. In the midst of this kind of world, we must ask ourselves the touchy questions of life—questions like, "What does it really mean to be in the world but not of the world?" Or, "Is it realistic to expect today's minister to take a vow of poverty, to expect his wife to serve macaroni and cheese to every visiting denominational executive, and to expect his daughter to buy her graduation dress at the church rummage sale?"

Even when the ministry is not involved, money is a controversial and confusing issue in our society. Some people insist that no sixteen-year-old needs a car—and that no family needs more than one—while other people say that the scriptural passages on materialism have to be understood in context and that a child of God should feel no obligation to settle for a secondhand refrigerator. It should not surprise anyone, then, to find out that opinions about money matters in the manse can be pretty diverse. And yet, overwhelming numbers of ministers' wives, regardless of denomination or geographic location, do seem to have fairly similar feelings about one aspect of this issue—the salary level in the ministry.

No Manna from Heaven

"The salary?" said one minister's wife. "It's the pits. I, myself, made three times more money before I was married." Many other ministers' wives echo this sentiment, often adding that people expect their ministers to have as much education as they expect their doctors to have without paying them anywhere near the same. A Northeastern minister's wife, in fact, noted that her husband (who has been ordained for twenty-six years and has four degrees, including an earned doctorate) makes only $12,500. And another minister's wife put it this way: "Sometimes unexpected weddings and funerals come at times when we really need the token money gifts, but I have always hated to be in the position of wishing for a funeral."

Other comments ranged from "very inadequate" to "pitiful," and the statistics seem to comply. For example, Mrs. John Lavender (Lucille), in her book *They Cry, Too!*, refers to a Bureau of Labor Statistics report on 432 occupations and points out that clergymen rank 316th. Although these men rank in the top ten educationally, she explains, they are in the financial bracket with cooks, waiters, and waitresses.[2]

Still, just saying that the salary in the ministry is not great is probably not, in itself, enough said. It isn't even enough to say that the majority of ministers' wives really believe that their husbands should be better paid. For, how many millions of lay people would be quick to reply, "Shouldn't we all?" It might be more helpful, therefore, to analyze some of the unique inconsistencies that the minister and his wife must face. And, we can probably do this most effectively by following an "everywoman" type of minister's wife through some of her everyday experiences. Let's start, then, by going back to the time when our fictional minister's wife was "such a beautiful bride."

Once Upon a Time

Wedding day! The bride is gloriously happy. She is marrying the man she loves; and, as an added bonus, that

---

2. Lucille Lavender, *They Cry, Too!* (Wheaton, Illinois: Tyndale House Publishers, Inc., 1976), p. 74.

man has a good education, a white collar job, and an elevated position in the community. Our everywoman thus marries her clergyman without a doubt in her mind, and she quickly settles down to enjoy some of the prestigious by-products of the ministry. Then the fateful day arrives—a chilly day in early December. Christmas is fast approaching, and the minister's wife suddenly realizes that she can't even afford the R.S.V.P. phone call for the gala charity ball. What can she do? Where can she turn? What happens when the holy honeymoon is over, and there is nowhere to go but to the free movie at the library—or to church? At that point, a minister's wife usually feels that there are only two possible alternatives. Either she can come unglued, or she can enter the first stage of coping with it all. Our everywoman chooses to enter stage one, the "I can't believe it" stage.

Stage One

Most ministers' wives can easily identify with the "I can't believe it" stage, because most ministers' wives have been there. "I can't believe we're struggling in the middle of this inflationary era, and people think we're getting discounts from the orthodontist," the minister's wife sighs. "I can't believe we live in the middle of a city, and everyone figures we're flooded with truckloads of fruits and vegetables all summer," she continues. "And I can't believe the minister is the only one besides the plumber who still makes house calls, and his salary is nowhere near that of the doctor (or come to think of it, the plumber)." How true. It is hard to believe any of these things. I can't even believe that my old high school steady who didn't go to college can afford a bigger home than my husband who has an entire office wall plastered with college recognitions and degrees.

Stage Two

Nevertheless, our fictional minister's wife must wave good-bye to the "I can't believe it" stage so that she can enter the investigative stage, for most ministers' wives eventually feel compelled to find out why all the inconsistencies exist. Our everywoman, therefore, starts thinking back to all the random comments she has ever heard people make about ministers' salaries. I, myself, have often done the same thing. . . . "It was depression time, and we just didn't have the money to pay the minister," my grandmother used to tell me. "And besides, the church people didn't want the minister to be tempted by too many luxuries anyway."

"But what happened after the depression, Grandma?" I would ask. "You have a color television set today, and you don't think there is anything sinful about that."

I never could get a straight answer back from her, but I always got the impression that she wasn't convinced that a man of God could handle an entire church and the antics of "Laverne & Shirley" at the same time. Many ministers' wives have heard similar comments, and most have also heard at least one statement that goes something like this: "That's the way we've always handled our minister's salary; and besides, we give him a free place to live, don't we?"

"Sure," our fictional everywoman sighs, "and we're also free to parade our leaky faucets in front of the Board of Trustees, get tension headaches whenever little Johnny tapes Mickey Mouse posters to the bedroom walls, and look forward to spending our retirement years in a barn."

Of course, it should be said that there is nothing new about any of this (and maybe that is one of the problems). Ministers' salaries and benefits have always been subject to a lot of church checks and balances, not to mention a few unbalanced checks. And clergymen's paychecks have always been dependent upon the foresight and consideration of their congregations.

I'll never forget the first time it ever dawned on me that my husband's monthly paycheck depends, to a large extent, upon the generosity of the members of his church. It was a mind-boggling thought. Still today, if I think about it too long, it can get pretty scary. Once I even found myself laughing hysterically just because I saw my spouse write "self-employed" on his IRS form. I was wondering if there has ever been a minister who was truly self-employed.

The unfortunate thing about all of this, of course, is the fact that there are those church members who don't understand the clergy salary situation at all. Some may even be suspicious of the minister's work habits and/or scholastic achievements. Often, these are the people who end up paying their pastors minimum wage and then locating their church parsonages in high-income neighborhoods. Not all church people are like that, however, so I don't really think it would be totally fair of our everywoman to spend all of her time blaming her husband's salary on the members of his congregation. In fact, I'm sure I'm not the only person in the world who has ever heard some clergyman say, "We know we got a real Christian for associate pastor this time because the fellow doesn't care anything at all about the salary."

Obviously then, lay people are not the only ones responsible for the history behind today's pastoral paychecks, which may be as good a place as any for our everywoman to end her investigative stage. She is not likely to discover much more about this low wage situation anyway; and the search, not for reasons, but for solutions, could very well turn out to be the more productive search in the end.

Stage Three

Thus, we come to the solution stage, stage three, a stage in which there are several possible directions for our minister's wife to consider. She could, for instance, take a look at rising meat prices and vow to turn the members of her family into strict vegetarians, but she would probably scratch this plan after having checked out the price of a head of cauliflower. In its place, then, she might settle on the idea of a low-key church campaign in favor of higher salaries for the staff....

Late one Saturday night, our minister's wife sneaks over to the church and tacks up all sorts of posters. "The elders who do good work as leaders should be considered worthy of receiving double pay, especially those who work hard at preaching and teaching (1 Tim. 5:17)." Or, "It's 2:00 A.M.; do you know where your minister is? He's on twenty-four-hour call again." For a while, this approach seems to have some potential, but it isn't long before our minister's wife realizes that the church people are simply skimming over her messages to get to the important ones. ("People whose last names begin with A–K are to provide the dessert for the church supper.")

Our everywoman is, therefore, forced to change tactics once again; and she finally decides, out of desperation, to start encouraging her husband to vie for a larger church. The boost-him-up-the-ladder approach sounds reasonable to this minister's wife until she finds it too difficult to ignore all those quizzical remarks about how nice it is that God always calls a minister upward to a higher salary. Before long, she feels too guilty to push. Then, just when she is about to give up and join some civic club that features soup lines, it dawns on her. "Why didn't I think of it before?" she shrieks. "I'm a capable, talented, semi-independent female living in an era of women's rights. I'll just go out and get myself a job, and everything will be wonderful." The perfect solution! Or is it?

In view of the large number of ministers' wives now in the job market, it should not surprise anyone to learn that our everywoman ends up juggling a home, a family, and a career, with the church tossed in as a bonus. But it also should not surprise anyone to learn that we must leave her there, for this woman's story is an unfinished one. She has chosen an increasingly popular kind of life, certainly, but she has also plunged into the middle of a complicated choice, a choice that symbolizes a whole new world for many of us.

Executive Mommies

When I was a little girl, I think I really believed that a mommy was someone who stayed home and vacuumed a lot. By the time I had graduated from college, however, no one seemed to know how to begin to define the role of mommy or daddy—or male or female, for that matter. Soon, contemporary women were charting all sorts of exciting new courses; and some of those women now feel happier and more satisfied than they ever have before. And yet, any woman who sets out to define the term *female* in today's world usually does find out that there is an awesome responsibility and quite a bit of risk involved in such a trek. This is just as true, and sometimes more so, when the woman in question is a minister's wife.

Ministers' wives seem to have varied feelings about their choices in life. Some, for instance, feel that they are being forced into the job market, that they are, in fact, selling out. These women don't seek employment because they want to buy an extra speedboat or even because they want to avoid afternoon church meetings. Rather, they work because they want to have heat in their homes next winter. They work because they live in a society that offers them few options beyond the two-paycheck family.

Other ministers' wives really want careers. These women find great fulfillment in their work, and they are thankful to be living in an era when they can choose to pursue careers without being hassled about it. How little hassle a minister's wife really does encounter, of course, depends upon a variety of factors, factors like her church, her choice of career, and the make-up of her family.

Issue: The Church

Church people are more likely to frown upon the working minister's wife with small children, although they might only grimace if she finds her work inside the church day-nursery. The real frowns, therefore, are often reserved for the minister's wife who decides to leave her children in that nursery and then go out to work somewhere beyond the stained-glass windows. And, trying to turn those frowns into smiles is seldom an easy task. It is not even easy for a minister's wife to decide what is best for herself and her marriage. For, although there are some very good arguments in favor of staying home with small children, there are also some very good arguments in favor of eating.

Issue: The Career

The type of career a minister's wife selects may make a difference too, although I have run across a few church people who would criticize just about any kind of job a minister's wife might hold. Once I was even asked if I thought my job as a department store buyer, since it was "out in the world," was an appropriate job for a minister's wife. (At the time, I didn't even have any children.) Since then, I have learned that my experience was not an unusual one—and that almost every minister's wife in the world has encountered at least one pulpit committee member who reserves his standing ovations for ministers' wives who announce that they are not career women.

Still, the type of one's job and the kind of church one's husband pastors merely form two small pieces of the entire jigsaw puzzle of life in the parsonage. In the end, the minister's wife has to make one big personal decision in order to fit the pieces together. "To whom do I owe my first allegiance?" I finally asked myself. "To whom am I really going to listen? Is it going to be my husband, my child, the members of my church, myself, the mailman, the dog next door, or any one of a number of other possibilities?"

Most ministers' wives, when asked about their allegiances, are quick to explain that a Christian's first allegiance must always go to God; and that is undoubtedly the easy, "A plus" answer. The difficult part, however, involves trying to put this into practice, trying to define it, and trying to pull out of it a direction in which to go. And, probably the most frustrating situations of all are those in which the church people don't echo God's leading for the minister's wife.

Yes, although it may be hard for a woman to give up a career for a baby she loves or for a husband with whom she is willing to compromise, it would be much harder for her to give up a career for a church tea party. Fortunately, many of today's churches are not asking their ministers' wives to do anything like that. Large numbers of working ministers' wives, in fact, report that they encountered no interference whatsoever from their churches when they decided to seek employment outside the home. Of course, some do; and it should also be said that the minister, himself, occasionally turns out to be a rather formidable obstacle.

Issue: The Spouse

Granted, the majority of ministers' wives probably go off to work or to school with their husbands' full support and encouragement, but we don't always hear the stories of how things got to that point—or how the peace is kept thereafter. We aren't always told how each minister learns to cope with society's not-so-subtle hint that the man should be the primary breadwinner in the home. And, I suspect that there are quite a few men standing in pulpits preaching dynamic sermons about not living by bread alone who would feel much less enthusiastic if their wives suddenly started bringing home all the "bread." Just ask any wife who makes more money than her husband. (A lot of them are probably ministers' wives.) Or ask the woman whose family entertains *her* business associates. Even the most enlightened male might require a little time to adjust to a situation like that.

Part of a minister's adjustment to a newly employed wife involves learning how to handle the day-to-day logistics of it all. And, early morning rush hour in a two-paycheck family doesn't even vaguely resemble the old, traditional concept of peaceful early-morning family devotion time. Rather, it may look more like a rerun of Cecil B. De Mille's Israelite Exodus. All of a sudden, everyone has to pack lunches and make breakfasts. Shared parenting becomes a necessity instead of an option; and, if Daddy has never before changed a diaper, this kind of switch in lifestyle can easily result in a classic case of family stress.

It doesn't have to be that way, of course. In fact, the ministers who are willing to "hang in there" with their working wives often say that the flexible hours of ministry turn out to be a real plus for them. And, while most people agree that a minister can't be expected to serve as a full-time sitter on church time, many ministers' wives say that it really helps to be married to men with flexible work schedules. I know what they mean. When my daughter was born, my own husband was able to squeeze a few pediatric appointments into his hectic, but flexible, schedule. Since he had been the oldest of eight children and I had been an only child (who had never held a baby until I held my own), his participation was the only thing that kept me from developing an extreme allergic reaction to motherhood. It has been over three years now, and I am still proud to be married to a man who felt secure enough to be the only male in a pediatric waiting room—in spite of the fact that he sometimes came home mumbling, "Why me?"

Whys and Wherefores

Why me? Perhaps it's not a bad question after all. It might even be a very healthy question for a minister's wife to ask as she searches for solutions to her financial problems. For, a minister's wife who asks such a question is likely to discover that she is not alone. She might also discover that few ministers' wives feel that money is the number one negative in the ministry—and that lots of ministers' wives who look for answers to their financial dilemmas end up finding them, often in the least expected places. There are many ministers' wives, for example, who have found that planning their budgets more carefully or devising ways to make a little extra money at home eases the bulk of their money problems. Others have plunged into the career world and found it to be a viable, even enjoyable, alternative to going broke. Still others have found that they are happiest staying home and accepting a standard of living that is lower than the one they once pursued.

Each person's choice must be an individual one, certainly; and no one choice is ever perfect. There will always be more struggles to face and more burdens to bear—like the struggle to understand God's will as it applies to one's finances, for instance, or the burden involved in coping with the new criticisms that will undoubtedly arise along the way. It isn't even easy to keep remembering to put more emphasis upon the business of living than upon the business of making one, although most ministers' wives know all about laying up "treasures in heaven."

Enjoying the Package Benefits

Admittedly, it takes a lot of ingenuity to learn how to handle the parsonage finances, and it takes a lot of work, too. But it is much more fun to watch Mrs. Pennypincher stroll into church in her new mink if you're not wearing her rejects; and the most satisfied minister's wife, in the end, is usually the one who has dug her way out from under that stack of time payments and started viewing life from a clearer perspective.

A clearer perspective. Is it really the crucial key to making ends meet happily in a parsonage? Most ministers' wives seem to believe that it is. One, in fact, responded to a question about the minister's salary with these thought-provoking words: "It's probably too low when compared with church members' salaries and probably too high when compared with the Master's expectations."

Moral :

It may be easier for a camel to go through the eye of a needle than for a rich man to enter the kingdom of God, but try explaining that to a bill collector—.

6.
The Lady in Waiting

A minister is a man who works twelve-hour days: a minister's wife is a woman who knows that anyone who questions that practice will be turned into a pillar of salt.

There is nothing easy about being married to a one-man band. Just ask any minister's wife. At the very least, her husband is preaching, teaching, counseling, marrying, burying, and doing a little janitor work on the side. Some ministers' wives try hard to accept their husbands' hectic schedules, asking only that their spouses join them for dinner once a week—at the church potluck. But such women often end up feeling rejected and lonely and depressed. Other ministers' wives resolve to go down fighting. They dress up in hot pink negligees and surprise their husbands with noontime romance. Or, if their spouses prefer to spend the lunch hour hanging around Arby's (looking for prospective church members), they set up private appointments through their husbands' secretaries. These women also try very hard; but they, too, often end up feeling rejected and lonely and depressed.

None of the preceding options sound especially appealing to me. A church dinner date would never satisfy me. If I were wearing a sexy negligee at noon, the president of the women's society would undoubtedly drop by. And, no one pays any attention to me when I'm depressed. I have, therefore, spent my first years of marriage looking for other alternatives, other ways for a minister's wife to combat the workaholic aspects of the ministry. One of those ways, which seems to have a reasonable amount of potential, is an examination of roots of the dilemma combined with an attempt to amend a few of them.

"I can't figure out the logic behind it all," I complained to my husband one day. "Other people work five days a week, and a minister feels guilty if he works only six." My spouse just mumbled something about going over to church to check his mail, and then he bounded out the door before I could finish my monologue. It didn't matter though. His actions had answered all of the questions I was going to ask. There is no real logic behind it all.

True, most clergymen do seem to start out with very honorable intentions. Some, for instance, begin their ministries fully determined to save the world single-handedly. Others, who are not quite so ambitious, just decide to save New York City. And I can understand this kind of enthusiasm. I, too, feel an overwhelming amount of gratitude for my own salvation. I, too, wish that everyone could experience what I am experiencing as a result of my relationship with Christ. And yet, that doesn't mean that I believe in a celestial genie who will grant my wish in direct ratio to the number of hours I spend wishing it; and it doesn't mean that I can't recognize a peptic ulcer when I see one coming.

Dealing with People

The origin of the ministerial ulcer can be very difficult to trace. But, at the very least, it is necessary for each pastor to know exactly how much he expects from himself—and exactly how much his congregation expects from him. "You're so lucky to have a husband who works only one day a week," a painfully naïve church member once told me. (She wasn't trying to be funny.) I held my tongue that day, but I must admit that I did give the woman an "expletive-deleted" kind of look. Instead, I should have thanked her, because I began, after that, to take a closer look at the people who actually believe that ministers spend their days playing golf.

Since that time, I've discovered that lots of people don't understand the ministry at all. Some even spend their entire lives paying preachers to do their own ministering for them. But why? Why do so many Christians so willingly shirk their individual responsibilities? Perhaps some of them are just lazy, but I suspect that the majority of them have been somehow conditioned to accept a sort of proxy representation of the Christian walk.

"Read Ephesians 4:11–12, and everything will be much clearer," I try to tell them, knowing full well that most of them have already heard lots of stories about how your coach (minister) is not supposed to run your own touchdowns for you. Many people simply don't accept such analogies, and I am not sure that this is the real crux of the matter anyway. For, a truly comprehensive study of the history behind a pastor's work habits would probably extend far beyond a study of the lay people in his church.

Dealing with the Self

The minister's job, according to the Ephesians passage, is to equip the people to do God's work; and the majority

of ministers seem to have no trouble accepting that fact—
in theory. The practical application of it is an entirely different story, however. Most of the ministers I know wind
up doing all the visiting, agreeing to lead youth groups in
their spare time, and acting as if they couldn't delegate
authority to the Apostle Paul. Try to talk to them about it,
and they say, "Wait until after Easter"; but Easter never
comes.

Could it be that ministers have messiah complexes?
Perhaps some do. Some may even set out to become martyrs, convinced that self-sacrifice is a large part of the job.
But others, for one reason or another, probably just expect
way too much of themselves. According to Christian
author/professor/minister/sociologist Anthony Campolo,
". . . studies have indicated that the congregations do not
have the same high expectations for ministers as the
ministers have for themselves. In short, they suffer because they fail to live up to their own expectations and are
constantly blaming their congregations for setting expectations which are too high for them."

Who? Me?

Why is the minister's drive to succeed such a strong
one? Why is it powerful enough, in some cases, to cause
migraine headaches, to destroy personal relationships,
even to mar the true vision of one's ministry? Undoubtedly, there are some ministers who work seventy-hour
weeks in order to avoid family intimacy. Others may allow
their competitive natures and their needs for affirmation to
get the best of them. Still others probably let their feelings
of self-worth get all tangled up in church growth charts.
And yet, my guess is that numbers of ministers push
themselves too hard merely because they are trying to
squeeze into clerical molds. They feel driven to meet all of
the needs of all of the people—and they figure that, in

order to do their jobs well, they have to be "faster than speeding bullets and more powerful than locomotives."

Stress is a popular word in our society today. We define it, measure it, determine its effect on our bodies, and offer courses on how to deal with it. We are told that time management is the key, that we have to find out how much stress we can effectively handle so that we can control our environments accordingly. We are taught that we can change our behavior and even some of our attitudes. But try telling all of this to a minister who is in the middle of a church building program, and see how far you get.

Oh well. Maybe it isn't that important. After all, ministers do have special guardian angels to protect them from the negative by-products of stress, don't they? Don't they? Whether we like it or not, they don't. In fact, many ministers' wives report that the common psychologically-induced illnesses are already running rampant among overworked clergymen. One such wife explained that her husband was once under so much stress that he got very sick. At the time, this minister was involved in a church that offered him little emotional support, and he finally got disillusioned enough with that church to leave it. Even then, no guardian angel ever showed up.

This is not an unusual story. And yet, I, myself, floundered around for a long time before I finally lost my own faith in ministerial guardian angels. I just didn't want to give it up. I didn't want to admit that my mother might have been right. ... Yes, I remember it well. While most protective parents send their children off on church trips only after those children have promised not to ride in cars driven by sixteen-year-olds, my own mother always told me I could ride with anyone but the minister. "Ministers don't even know there is a speed limit," my mother would say. "They think that they have special exemptions and special kinds of protection." I thought she was crazy at the time; but, years later, I found out that some ministers actually do live as though they had nine lives. I also found out that God really does allow his ministers to work themselves sick if they so desire.

Unfortunately, a sensitive, caring person who enters the pastorate automatically becomes a prime candidate for overwork. Some people attribute this fact to the lack of criteria by which to define success in the ministry, the idea that ministers work too hard because there is no way to measure their work. And it is true that people who are trying to motivate other people can't possibly chart their progress as easily as a businessman can chart the sale of vacuum cleaners. Even the ministers who do try to devise concrete methods of evaluation often end up doing little more than counting things (people in pews, money in collection plates) and recording empty numbers—and success really can become a minister's elusive numerical dream. But this is not, by any means, the whole story.

Also involved in a minister's drive to succeed is the fact that some pastors truly do love their work. "What more could anyone want?" my own husband said to me one evening. "I'm doing exactly what I love to do, and I'm getting paid for it."

"You're not getting paid much," I laughed, but I know what he meant. I know that my spouse really does enjoy his work. He even enjoys camping out with the junior high youth group, strange person that he is. Luckily though, he doesn't love his work too much to come home, because camping out in the church office is quite another issue in most ministers' homes. And it has certainly been known to happen. There are some ministers whose work schedules actually do get way out of hand. What happens then? What, if anything, can the minister's wife do to help?

Logs before Specks

When my husband and I honestly began to communicate about our work habits, I first had to admit that I had little right to complain. Not because a minister's heavenly work is exempt from earthly controls; but because, at the time, I was running a twenty-four-hour box office myself. Many nights, I would start typing the church newspaper as late as 10:00 P.M. simply because I had spent the rest of the day writing it. One day, it all stopped being fun.

I have heard so many sermons about how important it is to live every day of one's life—about how it is a person's duty, not to live long, but to live well. I have always listened carefully to those homilies (in spite of the fact that most of the ministers who were delivering them were not practicing what they were preaching), but I seldom took any of it very seriously. I couldn't. I needed to keep my conscience clear so that I could go home and bury myself under my mound of church newspapers. Needless to say, in those days, I wasn't living well at all; and, at the rate I was going, I am not sure I would have lived too long.

"I've spent hours of precious time typing the minutes of these meetings," I said to myself one day, "and next month they will be filed under 'old business' and forgotten." Add to that the fact that, even forty years from now, I will still be able to close my eyes and see... my daughter's first smile... my husband's tenth anniversary kiss... my friend walking that aisle at church, and it is easy to see how mixed up my priorities were. I was, as the saying goes, majoring on minors.

Testing the Brake Shoes

When I decided to make some changes in my work habits, I became determined to pour my efforts into things that are truly important to me. I also decided to slow down, even if it killed me. First, I rediscovered the fun of viewing the world from the top of a playground seesaw. Next, I took time out to count the colors in a rainbow. Then, I spent an afternoon introducing my daughter to a whole new, gloriously messy world called "fingerpainting." Soon I was getting the hang of it. In fact, it wasn't long before I felt proficient enough to begin converting my minister husband to my new way of life.

I am fully aware of the fact that ministers don't "convert" easily, so I never expected my busy spouse to drop everything and rush home to sign up for my first lecture on "How to Loosen a Clerical Collar." I did expect a decent amount of enthusiasm from him though. I guess that is why I was so shocked to learn that he didn't even want to audit the course. At first I tried to wait him out. "Just give him time," I told myself, but I eventually ran out of ways to rationalize my empty classroom. Before long, I knew I would have to start looking for other ways to handle the task of living with a workaholic minister.

It Is Not Good that the Woman Should Be Alone

Some non-workaholic wives who are married to workaholic ministers finally decide to become joint workaholics with their spouses. The "can't beat them, join them" method would never work for me, but it seems to work pretty well for many of them. One Illinois minister's wife, for instance, said that she and her husband now make everything a sort of joint project. "While he writes his sermons, I edit the church cookbook," she explained, and maybe there is something to be said for the side-by-side approach to work. At least you could plan some very interesting coffee breaks, and many of the ministers' wives who choose this method do say that it teaches them how to fill their own time with meaningful pursuits.

Other ministers' wives prefer a more indirect approach. They try to lure their husbands away from church with porterhouse steaks and chocolate mousse. A wife who selects this approach, of course, has to figure out how she is going to afford steak; and she also has to find some way to deal with the stigma against using worldly things to entice a man who has an "otherworldly" job (the old "mess with a minister's holy calendar only at your own risk" argument). Pretty difficult tasks, to say the least. But again, this may work for certain people.

The ministers' wives who find that both of the preceding methods are wrong for them usually begin searching for something in between. As a result, many of these women end up coping with their husbands' work habits by embarking upon the lifelong process of affecting change in those habits little by little. Ask them why they believe that a wife has the right to get so involved, and they explain that they have seen too many clergy marriages enter the danger zone—and heard too many ministers' wives cite "lack of time together" as the primary cause. They have, therefore, concluded that it is necessary for them to step in and lighten the burdens their workaholic husbands bear. "We have to try," they finally decide, "but where should we begin?"

"With all of those meetings!" exclaim about 90 percent of all ministers' wives. "With all of those Mickey Mouse meetings!" the braver ones declare. The volatile meeting issue—through the years, it has been the subject of many a bitter argument in many a manse. What minister's wife, for instance, doesn't know exactly what it feels like to spend her husband's fifty-minute break between meetings sitting at the dinner table giving everyone a bad case of indigestion by complaining about the situation? And yet, although it may be best to avoid mixing hostility with hamburgers, most ministers' wives believe that it becomes essential, at some point, to address the precarious meeting issue.

Step #1: Communication

Sometimes, when a minister and his wife discuss the meeting issue, they discover that many of their arguments revolve around the fact that the wife is simply not a meeting-oriented person, while the husband is. Getting feelings out into the open, thus, becomes an important task; and although this may not be an easy thing to do, it certainly beats sitting home alone throwing darts at old church bulletins or drowning one's sorrows in a box of chocolates.

There is another bonus involved in the communication approach—couples who decide to openly discuss their feelings are probably going to be more open to some compromises, too. The husband, for example, might admit that some of his meetings really aren't as important as a summit conference after all; and he might, therefore, agree to scratch or combine a few of them. The wife, in return, might agree to share dinner on the run a couple of nights each week. Before long, the couple could be well on their way toward finding an acceptable resolution to their problem.

I'll never forget the day my own husband and I finally struck a bargain on the meeting controversy. We were sitting on the couch reading books (between meetings) when my spouse suddenly looked at me and said, "I just thought of something. Most of the meetings I attend are meetings to plan meetings." I had been telling him that for years, of course; but I always use the words "I told you so" only as a last resort.

"What are you trying to say?" I replied, and by the end of the conversation we had agreed to a compromise. My spouse had agreed not to get angry whenever I inquire about his work schedule (as long as I don't inquire too loudly), and I had agreed to learn how to inquire more softly. It was a compromise most ministers' wives would readily accept, because most ministers' wives can find all sorts of subtle ways to get their points across.

One wife, for instance, might pin little notes to her husband's shorts: "The guardian angel assigned to you is not licensed to protect against high blood pressure"—or "She

who waits upon a minister should renew her library card."
Another wife might tuck a goal-setting book into her husband's attaché case—or slip a multiple-choice quiz into his
mountain of mail. "Someday," the quiz would read,
"your little Bobby is going to grow up and leave home. In
which of the following ways do you want him to remember you? (a) With pity, because Daddy was either not
at home or on the telephone. (b) With a deep and abiding
love for a father who truly knows how to enjoy a son. (c) I
don't care. I have to write my sermon now."

Ministers' wives who find this sort of thing too whimsi-
cal can choose other reminder tactics. Regular family dis-
cussions perhaps, or periodic evaluations of the kitchen
calendar. Some couples even go out to brunch together
once a week just to offset some of the time they spend
apart. Others recommend recreation with a purpose.
"Many times without planning," one Methodist minister's
wife explained, "our supper has been taken from the stove
to a nearby park so that we could picnic and romp our
short time away with the children."

Still, it should be said that any change in anyone's lifestyle is likely to be a very gradual change, no matter what
kind of approach a family may choose. For example, my
husband and I have spent a lot of time negotiating the
day-off issue, and there are still those weeks when he
conveniently forgets to take one. Naturally, I generally
confront him with his "oversights"—and he generally offers me the kind of explanation that would sound completely unintelligible to most people and perfectly normal
to any minister's wife. "But I was sick a day this week," he
said one time. "Doesn't that help?"

Step #2: Patience

Yes, it takes a lot of love and a lot of perseverance to live
with a minister. For, even a minister's wife who insists

that her husband is not a workaholic will usually admit that he does have to cope with fairly generous doses of stress in his work and that he is fully capable of performing the magical feat of leaving his mind at church when his body is at home. It is not surprising, then, that large numbers of ministers' wives recommend "getting away from it all" on a regular basis. Mrs. John Bisagno (Uldine) of the First Baptist Church in Houston, for example, said that a minister's wife must handle stress in the same way she would if her husband were in any other line of work. "Get away from the stress, or do something else for a little while," she said.

Many ministers' wives agree, and lots of them also talk about the importance of "rest and recuperation" at home. "I feel that I must make our home a place of calm and respite from the storms that rage in the world," a Baptist minister's wife explained. "It should be a place where my husband can experience renewal—a kind of 'filling station.' Am I succeeding? I like to think that I'm batting at least .500."

A batting average of .500 probably doesn't sound bad to most ministers' wives, especially since the long, slow process of building a good home life in the parsonage is seldom a simple, one-dimensional job. Sure, you can hang a "Happy Home" plaque in the family room, and you can keep Thursday nights free to play catch with Johnny. But what happens when no one is around to use the family room—or Johnny doesn't feel like playing catch on Thursdays? In today's world, it takes a lot of flexibility and a lot of creativity for a minister and his wife to build positive family relationships and also continue to do justice to their work. It takes a lot of time too.

People need time to build up the courage to question their habits and their ways of life. They also need to call time-out occasionally—to see, for instance, what would happen if no one (including the minister) agreed to chair this year's church Raspberry Bazaar. Some clergy couples even need to set aside time to list their priorities or to regularly ask themselves, "Why am I doing this?" Even learning how to relax takes time. It is too easy to forget how to dangle your feet in a stream and think of nothing but the ripples in the water. And it is too easy to forget that those special kinds of restorative moments stolen from a busy day are, in fact, the moments that actually give flavor to all the rest.

Sure, the planning meeting for the church canoe race may be a meeting worth attending, but it must never be confused with the task that Jesus calls us to perform. For, as Christians, whether we be ministers or not, our task is one of loving and nurturing, of building relationships with the people around us, and of pointing those people toward their God. And, in order to perform that task well, we do have to know when to end the meetings. We have to know when enough is enough.

Worth the Wait?

Sadly, many of the ministers I know always look like they are running to catch trains. "What kinds of earth-shaking secrets do they carry in those important-looking briefcases?" I used to ask myself. Then one day I found out... some posterboard, a few pieces of chalk, maybe the Sunday comics. That's about it. I was understandably confused. I needed some answers, so I began to ask some questions. I started by asking people to tell me about their favorite ministers—and I fully expected to hear stories about wonderful sermons, fantastic prayers, and inspiring Bible studies. Little did I know it then, but I was on my way toward finding out just how naïve my expectations really were.

"I'll never forget the day the pastor helped me put a light bulb in the overhead projector," a dedicated Church

School teacher said to me, and I was even more confused than before. "A minister certainly doesn't need to be a talented speaker or a Bible scholar to replace a light bulb," I reasoned, so I decided to interview someone else.

"I remember so vividly the day he noticed my four-year-old's homemade necklace," a middle-aged woman explained. "He even kneeled down and asked her all about it." Needless to say, it was hardly the kind of kneeling I had in mind.

"And you, sir, what do you remember most about your favorite minister?"

"The trash."

"The trash?" (I couldn't figure that one out at all.)

"After the annual church breakfast," the silver-haired man continued, "the Reverend stayed around and helped me take out the trash."

"Oh," I replied, still not getting the point, "were there lots of heavy loads?"

"No, just two cans."

"Two trash cans!" I exclaimed. "You could easily have carried two trash cans all by yourself. What in the world is so memorable about that?"

"We talked," the man said. "We really talked while we took out that trash, and you could never know how much I needed to talk that day."

My husband and I used to argue over who should take out the trash, but we don't do that so much anymore. I think we have gotten better at noticing the lonely people around us too, whether they be strangers, church people, neighborhood friends, or members of our own family. At least I hope we have gotten better at it, because I know for a fact that there have been times in the past when we were "too busy" to help anyone take out the trash. And I know that neither my husband nor I ever want to be *that* busy again.

A minister's wife might agree to play the waiting game on occasion, but she never has to play to lose—.

7.

To Love, Honor, and Endure

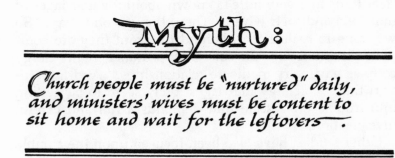

Myth:

Church people must be "nurtured" daily, and ministers' wives must be content to sit home and wait for the leftovers.

"Why doesn't Jenny's daddy live at Jenny's house?" my three-year-old asked me. "You mean you live with *both* of your real parents?" a teen-aged neighbor asked her friend. "Is there any way, in a world so saturated with change, for anyone to expect to stay married to the same person for life?" society asks us. Yes, the holy bond of matrimony has lost a good deal of its cohesiveness in our world today. And, although there are lots of people who still talk about the sanctity of the marriage relationship, divorce has become a common element of our present culture. This is perhaps most blatantly exemplified in the fact that a number of ministers are now getting divorced.

There are all kinds of statistics in all kinds of magazines these days. You can easily find out how many people use roll-on deodorants or how many cats prefer a name brand of kitty litter. There is very little statistical information about clergy divorce though, for so many of the ministers who get divorced end up leaving the ministry and, thus, leaving the clergy statistical charts. And yet, there are many authorities who do seem to feel that a number of clergy marriages are in trouble today.

In their recent book, *What's Happening to Clergy Marriages?*, well-known marriage counselors David and Vera Mace make this statement: "It became more and more clear to us that very little is known about the marriages of ministers and their wives." Then, they go on to say, "So we came to realize that, behind the front they are compelled to put up for the sake of appearance, many clergy couples have very mediocre relationships." And they report that "... clergy marriages today seem to be getting into trouble on a scale that demands a full and careful investigation."[3]

Other studies have also been focused upon the trouble in clergy marriage. Among them, a 1979 report put out by a task force of the United Methodist Church cites "new signs of stress in parsonage families and a growing readiness to see divorce as a solution to chronic strife in the home."[4]

Getting Here from There

This is a whole new ball game for many of us. When I was growing up, for example, it would never have crossed my mind that a minister and his wife might get divorced.

---

3. David & Vera Mace, *What's Happening to Clergy Marriages?* (Nashville: Abingdon, 1980), pp. 21 and 27.

4. Task Force on Clergy Divorce of the Council of Bishops of the United Methodist Church, *Handbook on Clergy Divorce* (Nashville, 1979), p. 1.

Clergy couples were just supposed to stick together for the duration, sort of like peanut butter and jelly. They were supposed to be happy together, too. And why not? They were the ones who had been singled out by God to know the joy of scooping a sinner out of the gutter—or teaching an unruly little sixth-grader how to sing "Jesus Loves Me."

As I look back on those days, I wonder how I could ever have been so naïve. All around me, I saw the signs of strain in lots of ministers' marriages. I was always able to pretend that the danger signals weren't there though; and, true to their roles in my contrived little dramas, all of those ministers and their wives managed to play their parts well. Most of them even laughed loudly enough and frequently enough to make my dream world seem totally believable. Today, I often wonder how many of those couples were depressed and miserable, struggling to accept their lots in life like twentieth-century martyrs, suffering in silence behind those reassuring Pepsodent smiles.

A Whole New World

Things are different now. Many of today's clergy couples actually are choosing to go their separate ways, and there are lots of factors involved in this. For one thing, divorces are now easier to obtain; and the church seems to have grown a little more tolerant of divorced ministers too. "Individuals are changing," a clergyman who has experienced divorce recently told me, "and, as individuals change, institutions change." This minister went on to talk about how he graduated from seminary as a divorced person in 1978. "Ten years before that," he explained, "I might not have been allowed to attend seminary at all. However, the changes have still not been sufficient enough to welcome me into the ministry as a divorced person. It is still difficult, in most cases, for a divorced minister to find a church; but in ten more years, who knows?"

It is true. Divorce probably is becoming more and more acceptable in all segments of our society. This, however, doesn't really explain why so many of today's clergy couples eventually find themselves considering it. It doesn't explain the reasons behind the splits. What, then, are those reasons? Why is there so much strain in ministers' marriages today?

Some people believe that the problems in many clergy marriages have something to do with the large amount of "divorce talk" in our society. Take, for instance, the woman whose friends start telling her that they wouldn't live one day with a man who attends a prayer breakfast every Saturday, works seven days a week, and eats crackers in bed. If they tell her often enough, she might very possibly start wondering why, in fact, she does. Before long, she might even start believing that she is the only person in the whole world still sleeping in such a "crummy" bed. Add to that the fact that the minister's wife in question is one of today's independent, capable females, a woman who actually could walk out on her husband if she really wanted to. If she really wanted to . . .

Call Me Ms.

The changing role of women is undoubtedly a very real factor to contend with in clergy marriage today. For, the kind of woman who is carving out a new niche in today's world is far removed from the kind of woman who would want to dissolve into a minister husband's "aura." And, in some ways, today's minister's wife is a brand new kind of woman. A few years ago, for example, no one would have expected a minister's wife to openly balk at the idea of moving to a new city with her husband. But many contemporary women have careers of their own to consider, and these women don't always celebrate their husbands' announcements of impending moves with pretty smiles and chocolate fudge cakes (baked from scratch).

"How can she do that?" the tongues begin to wag. "It is almighty God who is instituting that move!" (Never mind that he is doing it through a somewhat less mighty, occasionally disjointed group of people known as the pulpit committee.) Some ministers' wives explain their resistance by saying that they, too, are struggling with God's leading in their own lives. They also say that they don't intend to walk around wearing navy blue dresses monogrammed with big red *B*'s (for bad little minister's wife) simply because they insist upon playing active roles in complex decision-making processes.

In reality, then, what is actually happening is that these women are suggesting that their opinions and those of their husbands bear similar weight. At the same time though, some of those husbands, being ministers, are used to having their opinions elevated to slightly loftier planes than those of mere mortal men. And therein lies the dilemma. The issue is not one of whether or not to give the minister's wife the floor. In most cases, she has already taken it. Rather, the issue is a question: Can the minister and his wife work out their differences, make the necessary compromises, and block out any undue interference from their church... or will they just decide to split? Sometimes, of course, they split too easily.

Me First

When I was in first grade, I remember pushing my way into the chocolate milk line in front of Danny Carter and shouting, "Me first!" I wound up at the back end of the line, after having sustained a rather strong reprimand to my own back end. "That's not a nice little girl" was the message, and I heard it loud and clear. For I was a child of the fifties; and, above all else, I did want to be a nice little girl.

Then I grew up, and I started to interpret the new messages I received from my world. I became a bona fide member of the "Me First" generation, and I heard everyone talking about doing their own things. All around me, people were insisting that my first-grade teacher's definition of "nice" was totally passé. Yes, this is the "Looking out for Number One" decade, and all of us are being touched by it. I am sure of it, because whenever I try to stop people to ask them about it, they are always hurrying off to assertiveness-training class.

Some individuals think all of this is bad. Others think it is good. Either way though, we need to know that messages like "Me First" and "I Am Woman, Hear Me Roar" have permeated our entire society and have affected each one of us in all sorts of subtle ways. Even in the church. Even in the manse. And I am not, by any means, insinuating that all clergy couples who choose to divorce are selfish people. Instead, I am saying that the whole climate in which we live has something to do with the increase in divorce among us. Of course, the actual problems that a minister and his wife encounter in their day-to-day lives, even the little "tops left off the toothpaste" kinds of problems, are the real catalysts that eventually cause the explosions that result in those visits to judges' chambers. Perhaps, then, we should look at a few of those.

But How Do You Feel?

There are some people who say that trouble enters the clergy marriage because ministers, being highly educated people, communicate with words instead of with the raw kinds of emotions needed to sustain a marriage. I don't know about that, but I do know that it is difficult for anyone to spend his day dealing with people's deepest needs and then leave it all at the office—and I also know that many clergy couples do find it hard to share negative feelings.

Once I remember my own husband reacting to my angry outburst of pent-up emotion with a calm statement that began, "I hear you saying...." I responded by hurling a plate toward the floor and yelling, "Did you hear what that said?" (Unfortunately, it was not until after I had made a fool of myself that I remembered we have carpeting in the kitchen.) Needless to say, I am not particularly good at fighting, so I am not sure I can blame any of the unpleasant incidents in my own home on my husband's ministerial reactions during skirmishes. However, I do believe that good communication is always the key to a successful marriage. Most other people believe this too. The hard part is trying to keep the clogs out of the communication channels.

Don't Bother to Wait Up, Dear

Of course, you do have to see your husband occasionally in order to communicate with him, and some ministers' wives report that they seldom touch base with theirs. "He either comes home after the test pattern has flashed onto the TV screen, or he leaves before any self-respecting milkman is up," many women explain, and I can understand such laments. Ministers and their wives don't even get to sit together at church, and everyone knows that the family that sits together stays together (or something like that).

And yet, even clergy couples who do spend time together can still have trouble communicating. They can, for instance, lack the spiritual oneness they need. Colleen Townsend Evans called this a "lack of tough commitment and little willingness to give a primary human relationship the time and energy it requires to nurture communication and oneness." And Ruth Graham put it this way: "If husbands and wives do not continually refer to the Bible as their 'reference point,' seeking to learn from it day by day and to apply it to their own lives, it is easy to be brainwashed by the news media, increasing hedonism in our society, and the overall idea that man's chief end is personal happiness rather than glorifying God and enjoying him forever."

It is easy for a minister to tell a couple, during premarital counseling, that they must pray and read the Bible together or that they must nurture the spiritual bond between them as they give God control of their marriage. It is not nearly as easy, however, for him to go home and climb to the spiritual mountaintop with his own wife, every morning, over a bowl of soggy corn flakes, . . . and on the run.

Yes, clergy couples who want spiritual oneness in their marriages really do have to work at it, against all of the contemporary world's odds, just as hard as anyone else; and sometimes the struggle does get very tough. "We don't reach out to God earnestly enough," one minister's wife explained, "but God can mend broken relationships. He did ours." Then she added, "I had a nervous breakdown, and we almost broke up. I am learning to be more open and honest toward people now, but it takes much prayer."

Pastoral Cover-ups

Attitudes can be stumbling blocks to communication too. Some ministers, for example, actually do manage to convince themselves that they are almost perfect. (Too many inoculations of "Great sermon, pastor" and not enough antidotes of "That sure was a lot better than last week's sermon, Reverend," no doubt.) They are unable, therefore, ever to become vulnerable enough to build good marriages. Other ministers have poor self-images (a common problem among clergymen, according to some people), and they may choose to hide behind flowery language and theatric handshakes in order to avoid dealing with their self-doubt. These ministers usually don't understand themselves or their outlooks on life well enough to develop truly intimate relationships with people.

Martha Shedd, when asked to comment on the subject of marital tension in the ministry, said it this way: "Lots of ministers are not good husbands. They don't put their wives and families first—ahead of other less important business," and many ministers' wives agree with her viewpoint. Some of these women say that their husbands wear clergy masks at home. Others say that their husbands are married only to the church, while a few of the more "descriptive" ones talk about "my husband, the blockhead who lives in the church office." And yet, a number of women also feel that ministers' wives don't succeed in sharing their own feelings with their husbands; and they, too, probably have a good point. I, for one, must admit that my spouse often accuses me of expecting him to read my mind, and I guess I sometimes do think that he should be able to. (After all, I can read his.)

How Dare They!

Other ministers' wives speak of other kinds of trouble spots in clergy marriages. Take, for example, Lucille Lavender, a woman who has spoken with ministers' wives across the country. She believes that there is an unverbalized dynamic in clergy marriage that causes many of the marital problems that exist in the ministry. "Most clergy couples," she explained, "do not get divorced because they 'fall out of love' with each other." Rather, she cited the dynamic of the husband/pastor being fair game for anyone who wants to pressure him or make demands. "The husband," she said, "is usually the 'hunted' by people, not the 'hunter' for God." Then she went on to add these words:

> The wife watches her caring, committed, idealistic visionary husband slowly change into a hurting, oft-times defeated, 'spiritual errand boy' (though others may not notice). Unknowingly, he becomes a pleaser-of-people, quite removed from his ideal as servant-of-God. Some ministers' wives are not constituted to stand by quietly and helplessly at such 'injustice' and loss of self-esteem.

And lots of ministers' wives do talk about the problem of being married to men who have to live with injustice and criticism. They say that this can cause real tension in a marriage relationship.

What's a Passage?

Another marital problem often cited by ministers' wives is the dilemma of facing the mid-life crisis, often in combination with financial troubles, overwork, and feelings of inadequacy. A number of women even say that this sort of combination is enough to make some ministers too vulnerable to the females they counsel. A serious problem, to say the least. And yet, no one ever said that turning the tide of marital trouble in the ministry is going to be an easy task. For, there never has been an angel in charge of the clergy marital bliss department, just as there never has been an ordination ceremony that offers a clergyman the promise of a happily-ever-after marriage. It is not easy for a couple to change and grow together even when their world is turning smoothly—and ministers seldom live in smoothly-turning worlds.

If the minister's wife finds herself under any extra pressure (if the church nominating committee has just asked her to teach the one-year-old class again, for example, and the richest man in town has just written the church out of his will because he didn't like her purple dress, and the Women's League president has just accused her of using red wine in her "Chicken Divine"), a single instance of her husband's tardiness at the dinner table may even be more than enough to tip the harmonic balance in the parsonage. This doesn't mean, however, that divorce is the only option available to the troubled clergy couple. It doesn't even mean that every minister who has an unhappy wife should be defrocked and sent out onto the streets to sell encyclopedias.

A Dose of Humility

True, a clergy couple may have to consider seeking outside help, and seeking it early enough, in order to save their marriage. They may also have to accept the old adage about a doctor, even a Th.D., not being able to "operate" on himself; and they may have to work hard at putting preventive measures into practice. But lots of today's clergy couples (some with the help of pastoral relations committees, support groups, counseling services, and/or marriage enrichment experiences) actually are proving that the happily married minister is not an extinct species after all.

Of course, working at marriage, help or no help, is always very difficult work. Often, it is even difficult for a couple to determine how serious their marital problems really are. That is why it is so important for a minister and his wife to recognize and understand the clues around them. Perhaps, for example, they have gone for days without really talking; or perhaps their life together is becoming little more than a daily grind. Perhaps they just never feel very good about getting up in the morning—or about going to bed at night.

A Short-sheeted Sex Life

Going to bed at night... not a bad place to start. For, most of us already know that marital tension usually does reveal itself, to paraphrase William Shakespeare, betwixt the sheets. And, many husbands and wives could also verify the fact that a couple's sex life is likely to improve as they begin to cope with other kinds of turmoil in their marriage; and, in turn, a healthy sex life makes it easier to deal with other problems. Does this mean, then, that every parsonage should be X-rated? Does it mean that we should be asking our church project groups to make "Do Not Disturb" signs for ministers' doors? I don't really know; but I do tend to agree with the underlying assumption that a couple's privacy is important, and I have always suspected that it wouldn't hurt anyone to have a satisfied minister.

No one seems to be arguing against my endorsement of a good parsonage sex life. In fact, as far as I can tell, most of today's ministers' wives would quickly agree that sex is an integral part of marriage. That is not the problem. Rather, the problem is that the dog is scratching at the door, the president of the women's board needs a key to the church, the baby is drinking the water from the flower vase, and dear Mrs. Smith has to have a ride to the doctor. "How in the world can I ever find the time or the privacy to jump into bed with my husband in that kind of clerical madhouse?" numbers of ministers' wives sigh.

Sometimes couples do have to work very hard to obtain the kind of privacy they need. Maybe that is why some people, especially the ones who feel that romance and dirty diapers (or romance and church business) don't mix, believe that regular Friday night dates are a must. Others prefer midafternoon dates, while some would be more than willing to wake up at 3:00 A.M. for a date. I, myself, have been experimenting with a new idea. I am now try-

ing to persuade my husband to include me in his list of
church members whenever he goes out visiting. I always
promise him more than a cup of coffee and a friendly
chat—I've even been toying with the idea of borrowing a
key to a friend's apartment—and I think I may be making
some progress.

A Parsonage Divided

Still, figuring out how to carve "together time" from a
ridiculous schedule is often beyond my ability, and the
way my husband and I use the time we do carve out can be
just as frustrating. I shudder to think, for instance, how
many hours of vacation time we have spent discussing
next year's church stewardship drive. Even when we've
agreed to refrain from shop talk for an entire evening, we
have been known to slip in an occasional reference to an
upcoming church family retreat. ("It doesn't count," we
rationalize, "because it will be held off church grounds.")
No matter how hard we try, sometimes we get so caught
up in church talk that we almost feel like we need pipe
organ music in the background in order to make love.

There are other things that can cast shadows over intimate time together too. Take the problem of hero worship
and/or "church groupies" for example. It is a very complicated issue, I know. When I was a teen-ager, I used to fall
in love with every guy in uniform—even the service station attendants. So, it doesn't surprise me that a clerical
collar affects some people the same way. And yet, learning
to live with this, as the wife who washes the collar, can be
a difficult and tricky business.

Obviously, it is very important for a clergyman and his
wife to let everyone know that they do have a solid marriage. And there are lots of ways to do this. A playful hug
slipped into the middle of the annual Easter breakfast can
do wonders, as can an honest, enthusiastic personal illus-

tration tossed into a Church School discussion of happy marriages. At least once, I even revealed my own feelings unintentionally. It happened the day a Church School survey came out of my husband's Christian Education office.

The survey was delivered to all Church School teachers (of which, being a proper little minister's wife, I was, naturally, one). On the survey were questions about the Church School programs, classes, etc. At the bottom, there was a space for additional comments. "The Minister of Christian Education is sexy," was mine. How was I to know that the surveys would go to the Church School superintendent, not to the Minister of Christian Education?

A positive outlook on life is essential to any marriage. For, many a marriage has certainly been smashed beyond repair by the kind of person who walks along a lush, tree-lined boulevard and sees nothing but the sewers under the curbs—or the kind of person who concentrates only on the dirty dishes and spilled milk in a marriage. "How can I make you change?" such people ask their spouses, and it really is the worst question anyone can ever ask. I know, because I used to ask it constantly; and it never worked once.

Luckily, I finally learned that there is also a "best question anyone can ever ask." And that question is, "How can I, while loving you unconditionally, help you become all that God created you to be?" This, of course, is the direct opposite of marital possessiveness (which is sometimes defined as recreating one's spouse in one's own image); and it is, admittedly, a pretty difficult way to live. However, it is a way of life that is always worth the effort it takes. For, in an age of broken homes, in an age when there is nothing even remotely accidental about sustaining a happy marriage, what better gift could a couple give to the people around them than a model for a good marriage?

Karen Mains echoed this thought when she said the "lack of Christian role models for different styles of marriage" is related to divorce in the ministry. Other ministers' wives also said that God expects a Christian couple to show the world that problems can be used to toughen, rather than weaken, a marriage. "Too often we give up instead of growing and stretching to meet the challenge," explained Mrs. Bob Laurent (Joyce), whose husband is an evangelist/author. "I have never considered divorce as an option, therefore the pressures of the ministry have drawn my husband and me closer together."

Endurance with a Pay-off

Perhaps we do give up too easily sometimes. Perhaps this is typical of our whole culture. An Ohio minister's wife who has worked with large numbers of clergy couples feels that it is. "Everything in the world today is based on feelings," she said, "but just as your commitment to Christ can't be based on feelings, so your commitment to marriage can't be based on feelings either. If it were, many of us would have poisoned our spouses long ago. Instead, you make a commitment in marriage; and you use your will power, not your ever-changing feelings, to keep it."

Thus, with an understanding of the work involved in communication, a determination to keep the communication channels open, a willingness to search out help when needed, and a good strong dependence upon God... maybe, just maybe, today's clergy couples will be able to turn the tide of marital trouble in the ministry.

Moral :

The tiniest chapters in the world can be found in too many ministerial self-help books under the title "The Clergyman's Family."

8.
The Taming of the PK

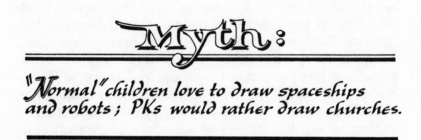

Myth:

"*Normal*" *children love to draw spaceships and robots ; PKs would rather draw churches.*

One of my earliest Church School memories dates back to a warm Sunday morning when I was sitting in a little country church. The song leader was especially excited that day because I, a visitor, had pushed the thermometer reading on the makeshift attendance chart to an all-time high. As a result, he began to belt out the opening hymn, "Love Lifted Me," with great enthusiasm. We never got past the first line though. For, as soon as we had sung the words, "I was sinking deep in sin," a little child with a booming voice scandalized the entire gathering by yelling out, "That's right! Whooopee!" Later I found out he was the preacher's kid.

I don't know whatever became of that particular PK (professional slang for preacher's kid), but I heard that he grew up to pursue a life of misdemeanor and was eventually forced to marry some girl at shotgun point. I was barely a teen-ager when I learned of that poor boy's wayward life, and I thought it was very sad. Today, I think the saddest part may be the fact that no one was surprised. Too many people simply shook their heads in a smug, all-knowing way and said, "That's a preacher's kid for you."

Not all of the PKs I encountered during my growing up years were alike. Some were openly rebellious, while others allowed themselves to be squeezed into various kinds of molds. A few ended up acting like push-button Pollyannas; but, even then, no one applauded their "good behavior" very loudly. For, good behavior was merely expected of them because they were preachers' kids. No matter what they did, they were in a no-win situation. Therefore, when I married a minister, I was almost afraid to think about the subject of parenthood. I wasn't at all sure I could handle being the mother of a PK.

The Die Is Cast

Eventually though, I did run across some well-adjusted preachers' kids; and, as time went by, I finally started feeling secure enough to try my own hand at raising one. I have never been sorry that I made that choice. However, I must admit that I have since learned more than I ever wanted to know about the fact that old traditions don't die easily.... The organ was playing softly when my husband and I, new baby in arms, walked toward the church altar. The dedication ceremony had officially begun, but my mind was not exactly on it. While the minister talked about how wonderful little babies are, I wondered how many people were going to expect my own daughter to be more wonderful than that baby over there in the second row.

"They won't if they get to know her," I told myself. "Surely not if they get to know her." For, my child (who hadn't even outgrown her "size 0" sleepers at that time) had already spit up on all my good blouses, tried to eat her teddy bear, kept her father and me up two whole nights in a row for no apparent reason, and, ooops, add one more, almost pulled the glasses off of the minister who was trying to dedicate her. Luckily, that particular pastor was the easygoing type. He calmly continued talking about raising children and about living a Christian family life. That is when my mind began to wander again.

"Could my beautiful little cherub somday become the church terror?" I fretted. "Impossible!" And yet, how many times does a child have to be told that PKs are bratty before he starts believing it—before he starts proving it? When the dedication ceremony ended that day, I walked out of the sanctuary very slowly. I sincerely hoped I could measure up to the challenge involved in raising a PK, but I wasn't at all sure that I could.

For quite a while after that, I continued to tread softly, half afraid to believe that my daughter was as normal as she seemed to be. "Is she organizing her little peers into a tricycle gang in the church toddler room when I'm not around?" I would ask myself. Then one day I did walk into her Church School class in time to hear her call little Suzy a dum dum, but I was quickly assured that she was not in the forefront with such language.

"Oh well," I finally sighed. "Maybe she is normal after all—and at least little Suzy isn't the daughter of the Chairman of the Board of Trustees." Soon after that experience, I stopped talking to myself about my child's normalcy. I decided, instead, to start concentrating on the extraneous factors—the environmental differences (both real and imagined)—that my PK might have to face out there in the real world.

Environmental Factor: The People

I have a friend whose five-year-old is always telling everyone that her parents are going to get married some-day. She also tells people that her mommy has lots of boyfriends. The mommy has been married to the daddy for a very long time, is as faithful as they come, and has no idea why her little girl dreams up such strange tales. She figures it must be a stage, and it probably is. And yet, stage or no stage, I cringe to think what would happen if my own little girl ever told a story like that to the wrong person. It is this kind of concern, then, that is one of the basic environmental differences between PKs and other children.

Environmental Factor: The Paycheck

Another environmental difference is the minister's salary level. For, while it is true that a preacher's daughter may not be the only little girl in the world whose parents can't afford to buy her a Barbie Dream House, she may very well be the only little girl on her block who is unable to provide proper housing for Barbie and Ken. Or, to put it another way, if the minister in question has moved his family into a "beautiful parsonage in a beautiful neighbor-hood" (where he has everything in common with his neighbors' intellects and educational levels and nothing at all in common with their weekends in Sun Valley), his children are bound to be the ones who stand out. And, on a scale of one to ten, most children would rate "standing out" at about minus eleven.

Environmental Factor: The Parsonage

Go one step further and assume that the minister in question is living in a beautiful, *furnished* parsonage. His children have an additional environmental difference with which to contend. For, they must, in many ways, live in a "look but don't touch" world; and, as a minister's wife from Tennessee put it, "Children and 'Duncan Phyfe' have little in common."

Of course, it should be said that the parents' attitudes toward money are the critical components of this particular puzzle, because a child will always remember his parents' feelings about their bank accounts much longer than he will remember how many times they couldn't afford ice cream. And, the messages about money that a parent conveys to his child often have little to do with the family's financial state. There are many people, for instance, who convey a "love of money" attitude to their children without ever having any money to love. Conversely, lots of clergy couples are able to raise their children to adulthood without ever letting the financial issue really become an issue. The subject of money—or the lack of it—does touch a PK's world, but it certainly doesn't have to control that world.

Environmental Factor: The Periscope

A PK is also touched, probably much more intensely, by the high visibility aspects of his father's profession. Sometimes his parents even encourage this, often unintentionally I suspect. A case in point: My husband was so thrilled to become a father that he kept reminding everyone that his wife had given birth to the most beautiful, intelligent baby ever born. It was typical new-fatherly pride, of course; but a minister is in a position to share his irrational opinions with quite a large number of people.

Even our daughter's first steps were announced from the pulpit, over the radio waves, for all the world to hear. I am certain that each person listening to the sermon that day had also taken first steps at one time or another (without benefit of media coverage, no doubt). Our child, however, was awarded instant celebrity status for stumbling toward a playpen and then toppling over it. Her actions were made even more highly visible than they needed to be. Of course, when my husband and I finally realized what we were doing, we did tone down our exaggerated accounts of our child's accomplishments. But we stopped, I think, just barely short of convincing her that the entire world revolves around her—having, therefore, almost succumbed to yet another one of the environmental differences.

Since that time, my husband and I have been using a more preventive method of PK-rearing, and we have decided that parents really can head off some of those tragic stories people tell about preachers' kids. Lots of ministers' wives seem to agree. For, although some of the ministers' wives who have small children do talk about feeling apprehensive, many ministers' wives say that they feel very good about the way their children turned out. One, for example, explained that she has always verbalized her firm resolve to disallow PK molds. She has always asked everyone to accept her children as human beings, "as people who participate at their own levels of spiritual growth"; and she believes that this has been largely successful. This woman is one among many who reported that their children grew up to be good, kind, loving human beings.

Environmental Factor: The Papa

Still, it is important to remember that the kind of preacher's kid a clergy couple raises probably depends, in large part, upon the kind of preacher who raises him. And this is not to say that every tack put on a church pew by a PK is "Daddy's fault" or that Mother isn't just as important in the home. Rather, it is to say that the unique situation in which a PK finds himself does exist because of his father's job and, thus, must involve the way his father interprets and performs the duties of that job.

"My daddy works every day of the week, even on Christmas," some ministers' children moan. "I made the mistake of giving birth on a Sunday," the minister's wife may add, "and my husband rushed nonstop from the labor room to the worship service." Sad but true. There are ministers who never slow down long enough to be fathers, ministers who are too busy changing the world ever to think about changing a diaper. Then one day, the future slips up and catches them off guard. It is an old story, but it is a story that continues to repeat itself over and over again. By the time the preacher gets ready to play with his daughter, the daughter has already laid aside her jump rope and is viewing the world from a loftier perch, a perch that no longer includes dear old Dad.

Sociologist Anthony Campolo believes that a careful analysis will indicate that ministers don't spend any more time fulfilling their vocational responsibilities than people in many other professions. He contends, therefore, that ministers do have time to plan creative activities with their families and to develop intimacy with them; but he further contends that they seldom do. If he is right (and in some cases it is obvious that he is), then why is this true? Why does it happen?

First, it should be said that it is very difficult to claim the freedom to be a real father in today's world. It is difficult to get out there and mix formula with the kind of dad who sees nothing unmanly about taking an active role in the child-rearing process. It is also much easier to preach about being a priest in the home than it is to practice that

Ephesians 6 passage. And it is simpler to add another meeting to the weekly calendar than it is to struggle with the task of combining a demanding career with the equally demanding job of being a father.

I remember sitting in one particular congregation when the minister's daughter walked to the altar and expressed her desire to accept Christ as her personal savior. The minister was noticeably moved. "May her Father in heaven never be disappointed with her father on earth," he prayed, and I found myself wondering how many fathers ever try to live up to such a prayer. Some time later, I was privileged to see my own husband take our little girl outside to view her first rainbow. He told her the Bible story about its origin, and he talked to her about God's promises. Again, I found myself wondering... how many women have husbands who take that kind of responsibility for Christian training in the home?

Yes, it is difficult to be both a good minister and a good father. Difficult, but not impossible. It simply took time for my own husband to learn how to be a father. It took time for him to really understand how important it is for both parents to "be there." Not just for those required-attendance family days, but for the common, ordinary, everyday moments of life, the moments where the real living is done. Take, for example, the first time my husband ever spent an entire day alone with our toddler. He ended up looking pitifully exhausted. "Before today," he told me, "I would never have believed I could get so angry at my child so quickly."

I started to say, "I learned that lesson a long time ago," but I didn't, because I could see the feeling of intense pride behind my spouse's grumblings. I could see that he was experiencing something new. Then, a few days later, when our daughter called Daddy on the phone to tell him she had used the potty chair for the first time, I knew for sure that he had "arrived." He talked with her and praised her and even thanked her for calling—and he was in the middle of a board meeting at the time.

How to . . . in No Easy Steps

I have never seen an authentic list of PK-rearing tips, and I imagine it is just as well. No one could ever devise a list that would be foolproof for all preachers' kids anyway. And besides, the most effective techniques are probably the ones that have little to do with the fact that the child in question is a preacher's child. For example, your PK, no matter how well he draws, shouldn't be praised for drawing Big Bird on the back of the man in the pew in front of him. This is not because Dad is the minister, but simply because it isn't good parental technique. For the same reason, you should sit down and answer your PK's most ridiculous questions, maybe even if the roast is drying out in the oven or the sermon isn't written yet. And, whether you work at a church or at a post office, you shouldn't say things like, "Tell him I'm not home," (when you are) or "I wasn't going over fifty-four miles an hour the whole time" (when you were).

Still, many clergy couples do have their own favorite PK-rearing methods, methods which have been tailored to fit the needs of their own individual children. Some, for example, suggest to their children that they should do certain things merely because they are Christian, not because they are PKs. One minister's wife even said she often uses the imperative, "Remember who you are," and then lets her youngsters interpret that however they want—"Child of God, Christian, member of good family tree, good kid, preacher's kid, etc." Another minister's wife added that her approach is "always spiritual, never vocational."

Several ministers' wives also reported that their families participate in regular family nights; and one Kentucky minister's wife, who has raised six children, talked in detail about the family council meetings in her home. She said that each member of her family always felt free to speak out in those meetings, and she added that there were usually eight different opinions on any given subject. This woman also talked about family prayer, as did a few others; but some ministers' wives said that there is just no way to fit regular, traditional family prayer times into their present schedules.

"After Little League practice is over and the bubble gum is cut out of the cat's paw and the dirty gym shorts (that have to be worn tomorrow or 'I'll just die') are washed, I feel lucky if there is enough time left to say a short prayer with each of my children at bedtime," explained one minister's wife, and a number of others seemed to agree with her. However, some of those ministers' wives did talk about involving their PKs in their busy lives. They said that they sometimes tote their children along to various community activities—or encourage little Jimmy to tag along to work with Dad on occasion.

The Consensus

Thus, each family is different, and each stage of family life is different too. One PK-rearing method may work well for one parent and fail miserably for another, and that is probably why there is so much difference of opinion whenever the discussion rolls around to the matter of living with a PK. Clergy parents do tend to agree on a few things though. Most agree, for instance, that their children don't need the extra burdens of church confidences brought home.

Yes, most ministers' wives seem to feel that it is hard enough for a child to grow up in today's world. They don't want to heap on any additional pressures. I would add to that the fact that a PK's parents don't need any additional pressures either. For, I know that I would hate to try to raise a little boy who is burdened with the worries of an entire congregation of people—or watch my little girl walk up to the leader of the Women's Circle and blurt out, "My daddy says your daughter takes the pill; I take aspirin when I have a cold too."

Many ministers' wives also seem to agree that they and their spouses are the crucial models in their children's lives. And they agree that living a normal family life, treating each family member as a unique individual, and encouraging the children to participate in activities they really like will usually cancel out any undue interference a PK may encounter at church. Lots of ministers' wives also talk about the quality of one's marriage being an important factor in the child-rearing process. And the quality of any marriage can be greatly improved if (in the words of a minister friend of mine) each person in that household tries to understand what the other people in that household need without always having to be told. This is particularly true of a married couple, of course.

Numbers of ministers' wives feel, too, that the lack of vibrancy and openness in a parent's Christian life can be a devastating influence upon a child, and I agree. I think that a child needs to see both of his parents (even the one who is ordained) struggle with their faith in their daily lives. I also think that the PKs who don't see this could very well turn out to be the ones who eventually decide that Dad's sermons on love and trust are way over their heads.

Besides, even small children are much too perceptive to accept hypocrisy in any form. I know, because I learned that particular lesson the hard way. It happened on a rainy Sunday morning, when my husband and I were yelling at each other about broken zippers and spilled oatmeal and last-minute reckless drives to church. As usual, my toddler was watching every move we made that morning... and I suddenly began, for the first time, to understand the whole scenario. "Yes," I finally said to myself, "Daddy may be a minister; but, many times, it is much easier for a child to believe that his parents are merely sinners saved by grace."

To Every Child There Is a Season

There are similarities and there are differences among all ministers' families. Some ministers have strict rules in their homes, while others have virtually none at all. And each child, being different, does react to his environmental circumstances in a unique way. That is why it is so crucially important for a parent to understand the growth stages that his children are passing through—to know, for example, that a young person who is internalizing his faith sometimes has to go through a period of rebellion in order to do this.

"I freaked out the first time Johnny stomped around and refused to go to church," one mother admitted, "and we all ended up looking like a Sunday-morning soap opera and solving nothing."

"How did you manage to survive it?" I asked her.

"Well," she said, "I finally calmed myself down by telling myself that it couldn't get worse."

"Then what happened?"

"Then it got worse. The children grew up to be teen-agers."

Yes, just when you have finally made it through your children's drawings of devils with pitchforks, entitled "What I Like Most about My Church," you find yourself face to face with a member of that dreaded species—the teen-aged PK—and you suddenly realize that you can't even threaten to take his crayons away anymore. Instead, you have to start trying to figure him out; and figuring out a teen-ager can be a very paradoxical task.

Few teen-agers, for instance, would ever admit that they want to grow up and become like their parents (even if they do). As a result, many teen-aged PKs go through stages when they would rather give up their telephones than go to church. Some parents are able to last out this sort of thing and eventually come out of it with some degree of willingness to go on living. A few are even able to keep their own roles from taking precedence over their children's development. These, then, are the parents who tough it out; and they are usually the ones who end up being the winners at the PK parent game.

When the Going Gets Tough

The game is tougher for some of us than it is for others. There is no doubt about it. One young mother, for example, talked about her husband being called to a church where there was no nursery program. She said that she was just too tired of spending six days a week with "diapers, tears, noise, and messes" to feel good about tending the church cribs herself. She wanted, instead, to get out and go to church on Sundays; but whenever she toted her children along, there was trouble. "A deacon visited me," she explained, "and he suggested not bringing the baby to church." This minister's wife wound up sulking at home with her kids all summer—and then leaving that particular church in the fall.

Another minister's wife told about being in a church where her children were subjected to intense pressure. They were treated "like second-class PKs," she said. They developed problems ranging from shoplifting to marijuana to tension-induced illness to disillusionment with the organized church—all complicated enough to be contributing factors in their father's eventual decision to leave the pastorate.

Even when the church environment is good, the task of

raising a child in a parsonage is seldom an easy task. Take, for example, the minister's wife who responded to the question, "Are you the daughter of a minister?" by saying, "No, thank God." She obviously knows how hard it is to rear secure sons and daughters in a home where no one can even promise that Daddy will actually be there next Saturday to see his youngsters perfect their starring roles as trees in the Westwood school play. And I know how hard it is too. There have already been many times when I have wanted to scream at my own baby, "You can't burp in the middle of the pastoral prayer! Your daddy is the minister!"

Preparing for Sudden Death Overtime

I still don't know what kinds of pressures the world is someday going to put on my own child, and if I think too long about the PK parent game it makes me very crazy. So, instead of agonizing over all of this, I have decided to put the emphasis on guidance and love. I will continue, therefore, to pray for my child and to show concern for her well-being; but I am also going to try to relax and enjoy her. I am going to try to treat her as an individual little person, too, and maybe that won't be such an impossible task after all.

A number of ministers' wives do say that their children have never felt any extreme amounts of pressure from their congregations. And they also say that most of the people in today's churches will not faint if they see the preacher's child pass a note in church or play tic-tac-toe on his bulletin cover. In fact, one minister's wife even explained that she never has to worry about molds, but only about the members of her church loving her son to death.

Could it be, then, that a child's PK status is not really the deciding factor in his development? I don't know. But, in the knowledge that no one, clergy or otherwise, is given a guarantee that he will raise healthy, happy, Christian sons and daughters, I figure that the most anyone can do with the "train up a child" directive is to prayerfully give it his best shot.

"Do we live at church or at home?" my daughter asked me one day last week, and I made a mental note: "We're spending too much time at church again. Got to slow down." Then, a little later the same day, a friend of mine said something that came out sounding like, "Wouldn't a PK really rather go to prayer meeting than eat chocolate ice-cream cones?" I suppose it was a rhetorical question, for I'm not even sure that a PK's dad would rather go to prayer meeting than eat chocolate ice-cream cones (and I'm relatively certain that his mother wouldn't). And yet, I found myself wondering how many people actually do believe that sort of thing; and it bothered me a little.

Occasionally, I even find myself wondering if anyone ever raised a normal PK; but whenever I do, something encouraging usually seems to happen. I run across a real-life, normal, adult PK, for example; or I walk into my daughter's room just in time to hear her carrying on a beautiful conversation with God about her paper dolls. And I always end up deciding that I do have a shot at it after all, if I can just keep remembering the essentials . . . the essentials—like the fact that a parent can interfere in his child's life too much—and the fact that I do have to spend time building a strong love relationship with my spouse if I want my child to "get it right"—and the fact that every mother and father must prepare themselves for that day when they will have to take one last glance backward and then let go.

I think I can remember. For, although I desperately want my child to be a Christian, I really believe that I want it to be her own choice even more. It can't be because Daddy is the minister. It just can't be. So, however painful the journey from here to there may be, I suppose I will just have to embark upon it—and I will have to try to be ready to say good-bye when my child's road forks away from my own....

"Mommy, help! Holly Hobbie stuck her tongue out at me when I asked her to say grace. I need you right now!"

"Coming, Becky."

Yes, I just may have a shot at it.

He who starts out raising a PK can end up with a mess, but only because he who starts out raising any child can end up with a mess.

9.

The Still Small Voice

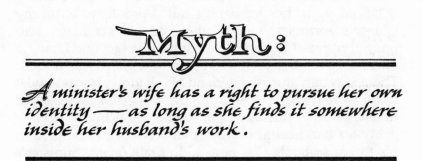

Myth:

A minister's wife has a right to pursue her own identity — as long as she finds it somewhere inside her husband's work.

Am I a minister's wife? Or am I the wife of a man who happens to be a minister? Or am I simply a woman who happens to be a wife? The semantics behind the role really bothers some ministers' wives. "We don't want to be known as 'just someone's wife,'" they explain, and I can understand that. I want my own identity, too. And yet, I generally don't mind having people introduce me as their minister's wife, especially since I know that those people almost always mean well. It is when someone introduces me as "our minister's wife, er, a, what's-her-name" that I am not quite so enthusiastic. Maybe not so much because

131

the individual forgot my name, but because he remembered my label.

At any rate, there are times when I feel like screaming, "Just wait until your kid needs a reference for his student work application and I sign it 'what's-her-name.' " I never do though. Instead, I usually just smile and pretend that I've spent many years preparing to be a nonentity—and I promise myself that I will someday find a way to inform the world that my wedding ceremony didn't end with the words: "And now I pronounce you minister and wife." (At least I don't think it did.)

I used to be one of those ministers' wives whose identity is bound up in her husband's call. I proofread all of my spouse's sermons, tagged along to his seminars, and poured coffee at his board meetings. The fact that I had no time left over for myself was irrelevant. There was no self. There was only the minister and his shadow. It was almost as if I were trying to blend into my respected professional husband. Then one day I got my big chance.

My husband caught a cold that week, and it settled in his throat so badly that he couldn't talk (every minister's most haunting nightmare). When Sunday arrived, I got to scurry around and do many of the things the minister normally does. It was a great experience for me because it helped me discover that I am not even faintly interested in being a pastor. Unfortunately though, by the time I got around to making that big discovery, I had pretty much forgotten how to be anything else.

Seek, and Ye Shall Find

I began immediately to try and take charge of my life, to pick up the church-stained pieces and to begin again. Perhaps this was a part of my coming-of-age process, the natural result of reaching a certain birthday or coping with a certain "passage." I am not sure. I only know that I finally did get around to asking myself the predictable questions: Where am I going? Why am I here? What do I really value? What is my life saying that I value? Why do I so often feel like I am just treading water? Who am I... really?

I think it sometimes takes a minister's wife longer than anyone else to get around to asking those questions. Maybe this is because the minister's wife is always too busy practicing the piano numbers for next week's mid-week service. Or maybe it is because, as a minister's wife from the Evangelical Free Church pointed out, many ministers' wives marry young, before they have had time to establish their own identities, and are often ripe for being squeezed into molds. I am not sure. I just know that I, myself, spent a very long time brushing off my toddler's three critical questions ("Who am I, Mommy? Who is Daddy? And who are you?") before I realized that I had answers only for the first two.

Playing Twenty Questions

When I was in high school, everyone was trying to find out who he was. All of my friends were sitting around doing a lot of what is now termed "navel-gazing." Some of them eventually "found themselves" in their rooms at home. Others had to hitchhike to California to accomplish it. I guess I was the exception, because I never really got into those kinds of introspection.

"Why should I?" I reasoned. "I know everything I need to know about myself and about life." Besides, I figured I could live a couple of lifetimes and never exhaust all of the little guidelines my parents and grandparents had passed along to me. "Don't lean back in the movie theater or you'll get ringworm," they had said. "And don't cross your eyes or they won't go back." And, "By all means, don't touch it, because you never know where it's been."

I even got married before I had learned to think for myself, and I lapped up the goals and ideas of my husband as eagerly as I had accepted those of my parents. That is when I finally became perfect at something. I became the perfect definition of the word "stereotype": One who is "lacking any individuality." Still, I continued to avoid making the transition to adulthood. I neither selected nor owned my values or my attitudes or my feelings. Then, much later, when I finally did get the urge to set my own goals and make my own choices, it dawned on me that I had lost my true self somewhere in the mix. In order to take control, therefore, I could see that I would have to try to get to know the person behind the painted-on smile.

The "Real Me"

A minister's wife from West Virginia explained her own plight this way: "The 'church me' is basically quiet, submissive—I smile and bake cakes on cue. The 'real me'—the 'me' that was free and creative and worked so hard in the church before I married a clergyman—is committed, has strong opinions, but hopefully is also kind and loving." She then added, "I view my role in the church as a crippling suit of armor—unhealthy for me and vastly wasteful for the church. What I would like, and am working toward, is to be a free and creative lay woman, a helper to my husband, surely, but not a shadow that walks silently in his footsteps."

Another minister's wife talked about how she once tried to please everyone in the congregation. She stopped when someone informed her that she would be surprised to know how much she was talked about. It was then that she realized how impossible—and how unscriptural—it is for a minister's wife to live a life that is designed to please all of the church people. And how true this is. For, no matter what you do, someone always wishes you had done something else anyway. Or, as one minister's wife put it, "The music director wishes you had a better singing voice, Mr. W. wishes you were more politically aware, boutique owner Mrs. S. wishes you were a better dresser, and Grandmother R. wishes you were a better mother."

When I finally decided to work toward building my own identity, I felt very exhilarated; but I also felt a little frightened. "What will it be like to cast off all of the labels and all of the masks?" I wondered. "How will I handle that agonizing moment in between the old me and the real me?" I worried that I might feel too vulnerable, too naked, too alone. Also, I wasn't sure where to begin my growth process. I knew I would never be able to stay quiet long enough to stand on my head and meditate. And, although I did find a few good books among the million or so volumes that line my husband's office walls, I also knew that lectures and self-help studies weren't the whole answer. As a result of all this, it took some time for me to discover that the best approach for me rested in open, honest observation of myself.

Getting to Know Me

Defining one's likes and dislikes and one's feelings and attitudes is always a difficult task, but facing those things can be a really harrowing experience. For example, I will never forget the day I stopped hiding behind my back pack and admitted that I hate camping. Hate camping? Yes, and retreats and overnights and anything that even vaguely resembles a tent; and I am fully aware of the fact that such a confession would sound pretty sacrilegious in some circles. I know, too, that it can be an especially dangerous confession to make if one's husband is a youth

minister (which mine happened to be at the time). Perhaps
that is why I pretended to love sloppy-looking "s'mores"
and soggy sleeping bags for so long.

There comes a time, however, when pretense becomes
unbearable. So, I finally did build up the courage to announce that I had eaten my last sticky marshmallow—and
that I had allowed myself to be zipped into my bed for the
last time. When I did, I felt surprisingly refreshed; and I
got a much calmer reaction from people than I had expected to get. I also found out that it is not always disas-
trous to tell the truth about oneself. And I thus began to
look for more truths. Before long, I was asking myself
what characteristics I really do possess, what kinds of
things I truly like to do, and how I can become the person
God created me to be.

Several ministers' wives have told me that they see a lot
of need-sublimation among their peers. They say that a
minister's wife can always find someone in the congregation whose needs are greater than hers. "Sure, Christian
servanthood is important," these women say, "But if Mrs.
Smith's bunions take precedence over your own needs too
often, you can get completely out of touch with your feelings. You can end up being no good for either Mrs. Smith
or yourself."

They are right, of course. It is easy for a minister's wife
to get too drained to practice the art of active listening, too
tired to hear someone's gripes about the weather and respond to what the person is really saying underneath. In
fact, it is very possible for a minister's wife to wind up
getting disgusted with certain attitudes in people simply
because she is too preoccupied to recognize those attitudes
as negative characteristics lying dormant deep inside herself.

"... love thy neighbor as thyself," my husband
preaches, but how many times have I listened to those
words without really hearing them? How many times

have I sat through sermons on that scripture passage wishing I weren't the minister's wife so that I could doze off without incriminating myself? More times than I want to admit, I am sure. And even when I do think about that particular concept, I seldom put much emphasis on the "love thyself" part of it and on the fact that feeling good about oneself is a prerequisite for loving others.

Consequently, there are days when I feel that my life is going nowhere. There are days when I think that no one ever appreciates me or notices my efforts (except maybe the neighborhood kids; and, even then, I often suspect that this has something to do with the bubble-gum machine in my kitchen). Sure, I know that I am a child of God. I know that I am a unique, invaluable human being. And yet, whenever I'm not using any of the abilities God has given me, I just don't feel very good about myself.

Step #1: Unwrapping the Gifts

I know many Christians who skim over the lists of spiritual gifts in 1 Corinthians and Romans and then announce that they don't have any gifts at all. This is impossible, of course, because every Christian has at least one; but many people never look at themselves closely enough to identify the gifts they do have. Take the extremely shy minister's wife, for example. She may spend years thinking that she is capable of doing little more than stuttering through a benediction. "I surround my 'thees and thous' with so many dangling participles that it makes me sick," she may groan, while her husband continues to pound the pulpit with authority and to deliver those holy goosebump-producing prayers on demand.

It is easy to see how a shy minister's wife could talk herself into believing that she has little to offer to the world, but it just isn't true. Such women, for example, often have enormous, sometimes untapped, abilities to listen and to love; and there are many ways to put those abilities to use. Ruth Graham talked about how a minister's wife can encourage people beautifully and freely. She explained that a minister's wife can encourage her husband, her children, and anyone in the congregation who might be needing it. And she said it is important to remember that "those who appear to need it the least frequently need it the most."

Many people are more creative than they think they are too. Or, at least they can become more creative than they think they can become. "I couldn't draw a straight line if it would win my husband a multi-staff church with 3000 members," some ministers' wives say. But an individual doesn't have to paint a masterpiece in oils or compose a breathtaking sonata in order to be creative. Rather, true creativity is simply an attitude toward life. It is the product of allowing one's mind the freedom to wander and to perceive.

There are many ways in which women show creativity without even realizing it. One may place a freshly-picked daisy on a troubled friend's desk at work. Another may add a raisin face to the top of her child's drab old cupcake—or tuck a sexy love note into her husband's sermon copy. In fact, being creative is often little more than being interested enough to ask questions and open enough to express oneself. And there are lots of people who actually work at acquiring creativity. Some of them keep notebooks handy and jot down touchy situations they encounter each week. Then they pencil in notes explaining what they could do (creative alternatives) to improve each situation. Other people practice the art of looking and really seeing, continually reminding themselves not only to stop and smell the roses, but to scrutinize each one of them, too.

Creative ministers' wives don't always have IQs of 150, and they don't always have college degrees either. Many of them merely plan into their schedules quiet times of thinking and praying, in the understanding that true creativity, for any Christian, comes from God. They also work toward developing attitudes of positive, creative living in all areas of their lives. And they try hard to remember that creativity is an integral component of God's plan for his people.

It is true. God could have constructed the Golden Gate Bridge or written *Jane Eyre* all by himself, but he didn't. The day I finally realized that God didn't leave the world unfinished just for the youth group I was chaperoning was a very significant day in my life. For, that is when I truly began to understand that every minister's wife has the potential for doing much more than saying, "Fine sermon, dear" or "Do you take cream and sugar?" Since then, however, I have also begun to understand that the ministers' wives who realize their potentials are the ministers' wives who have broken free from all of those smothering molds.

Step #2: Using the Gifts

Ministers' wives who declare independence day in the parsonage often do so in "fear and trembling." I suppose this is because it seems so easy to remain dependent, to piggyback upon someone else's interests. It seems less risky, for example, to forfeit one's vote at a controversial church meeting than it does to let one's congregation see and respond to the real woman behind the baby grand. Of course, many of the risks that we so carefully avoid may not be as real as we think they are. Just ask one of the many ministers' wives who contend that revealing one's real self to one's congregation is the most positive step any minister's wife can ever take.

Granted, there are some church members who don't understand a minister's wife's need to be herself, but there are also large numbers of people who are too busy struggling with their own problems to worry about proper protocol for ministers' wives. Sure, there may have been a time when a minister's wife who switched pews on Sunday would have been gossiped about, but most of today's ministers' wives have already gone much further than that. And besides, every minister's wife eventually has to make her own decision about which voice she is going to heed anyway—and that still small voice is always there for any Christian who draws aside from the noise of the television set long enough to hear it.

Of course, it should be said that there are many different kinds of ways to assert one's individuality. Take, for example, the minister's wife who walks into a church business meeting with a negative attitude. She is probably not going to gather a great deal of support for her cause. Conversely, the minister's wife who is considerate and flexible, the minister's wife who has a positive attitude about Christian service, and about Christian love, is much more likely to discourage needless criticism.

Also, individuality and independence mean different things to different people. To some, this may mean a career. It may be that some highly educated, highly skilled ministers' wives have real needs to use their abilities outside the home. Not all ministers' wives feel that way though. For others, being oneself may mean being able to take pride in a load of laundry without feeling that having a green (or blue) thumb with a bottle of bleach is a worthless talent. That is why some ministers' wives feel the desire to return to school and work on new degrees, while others find complete fulfillment in community activities and in spending time with close friends. And, it is why some ministers' wives want to feel strong enough to say yes to the pilots' licenses they always wanted to get, while others only want to feel strong enough to say no to the organs they never wanted to play. (Ah yes, lots of ministers' wives end up talking to organs.)

Step #3: Getting It All Together

Education, skills, social activities—these can be very helpful tools for the minister's wife to use in forming her own identity. And yet, the fact does remain that they are only tools. No matter how much education one has, for example, it cannot guarantee a trouble-free life. (My husband spent twenty years in school, and he still can't seem to read my "bring home a quart of milk" notes.) And no matter how successful one's career may be, it can't promise total contentment. Even having lots of friends doesn't make life perfect, because there is only one way for a person to ever truly find himself; and that, of course, is by discovering life's real meaning through the person of Jesus Christ.

Yes, I know. That sounds a little bit like a sermon, and another sermon is precisely what most ministers' wives could easily live without. But it really is true. God's help does make the difference, even for a minister's wife. At the same time though, God doesn't promise anyone a smooth road to travel. In fact, it can be very painful to find out that, in many ways, no one is going to take care of you except you. Perhaps that is why some ministers' wives never do come to grips with that particular truth.

A minister's wife whose husband works with a denominational insurance program talked with me about the number of depressed ministers and wives, and she explained to me that many people honestly believe that someone else is always going to take care of them. It simply isn't true, of course. "Social Security isn't going to take care of all of your needs," my friend told me, "and your insurance policies aren't—not really. Even your husband can't, not if you don't take care of yourself." And yet, many people still want to believe that relationships or jobs or charity work can fill all their needs and make them completely happy. Many people get caught in the trap of assigning to their activities or to their roles all kinds of impossible expectations.

One very wise young woman, whose husband is planning to enter the seminary, talked with me about her own expectations. She said that she expects the ministry to offer her a good life. "Not necessarily because of the ministry," she said, "but because I want a good life." Then she added, "If Jeff were still working at the grocery store, then I would expect a good life there, too, because it is me doing the Lord's will that offers me the good life."

I wish I had been so wise. But, amid the commotion of stewardship programs and coconut cakes and car washes, it is just too easy to forget. It is easy to forget that being independent simply means claiming the right to lead one's own life in union with God. It is easy to forget that one must continually yield oneself to Christ in order to make this work. And it is easy, particularly in a world filled with so many misunderstood concepts of liberation, to forget that true freedom always contains a large dose of obedience.

Decisions, Decisions

Losing oneself to find oneself has never been a simple spiritual truth to grasp. This is probably because too many people try to lose themselves, not in the supreme Lordship of God, but in things or in other people—and it just doesn't work that way. Not even a minister with a balanced church budget and an overflow congregation has the power to make his wife happy. Only she holds that power. Only she can decide what her attitude toward her life is going to be.

"I believe my attitude is extremely important," explained one minister's wife, "for the atmosphere I create encourages my husband to minister or discourages him to the point that his vision fades." And another minister's wife, who happens to be deaf, told of her struggle to be a whole person "despite being a minister's wife and despite being deaf." She expressed her feelings this way: "I have felt stigmatized, but I realize that was a feeling *I* gave me. I needed to create my place within the area given me." Then, she explained that she now has a sense of self—and that her "now" reasons for marrying a minister would be better than her "then" reasons were.

Of course, many of the ministers' wives who are trying to assert their own personhoods do talk about having to learn how to walk some very fine lines. "In some situations," such women say, "speaking out is just not worth the risk." There are other situations, however, where those same women are more than willing to take the chance. In fact, one minister's wife, whose husband was called to a church where all women automatically became members of a church women's group, even dared to write a letter of resignation to that particular group. Many ministers' wives might disagree with such an approach, but this woman felt strongly enough about that specific church practice to take action against it.

Tuning into God's Words

Lots of us are taking action against different things in different ways these days, and maybe those actions are justified more often than not. Maybe we are headed in the right direction after all. And yet, it is so important to remember that one's desire to proclaim one's freedom must be tempered with a lot of prayer and an overabundance of love. For, it is the task of every minister's wife to learn how to re-examine and to revise, to be open to a balance in life, and to understand that it is possible to write too many letters.

"The main thing that has helped me to 'hang in,'" explained a Florida minister's wife, "is the thought that I represent Christ to many who are on the verge of committing their lives to him." It is, admittedly, a very heavy responsibility. And, unless great care is taken, it is entirely possible for a minister's wife to lose herself in order to find herself only to lose herself once more.

Moral:

There is a middle ground between playing adult hide-and-seek and becoming the church's resident Don Rickles.

10.
Get Thee Behind Me, Stereotypes

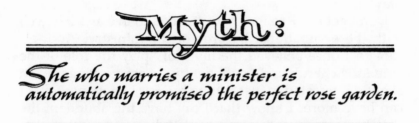

Myth:

She who marries a minister is automatically promised the perfect rose garden.

Contrary to popular opinion, a minister's wife is not called to the podium during her husband's ordination ceremony and presented with a first-class ticket entitling her to a long, easy plane ride to heaven. In fact, numbers of ministers' wives would probably describe their journeys through life in very unheavenly terms. Some might even say that they have been taken on bumpy jeep rides directly to jail—without passing go and without collecting $200.

My own jeep ride used to be bumpier than it is today, because I now feel reasonably comfortable with my chosen role in the church. And yet, there are still days when I have trouble coping with it all. There are days when I need to be counseled and have to play "Who Do You Trust?" (A minister's wife can't even call dial-a-prayer because she's never sure whether or not it's her husband's week to man the phones.) There are days when I look at my impressive collection of religious mementoes and long for a slightly risqué birthday card or a gift box that contains something other than a cross that glows in the dark. And there are days when I wish I weren't always on display. Sometimes, in fact, I even toy with the idea of wearing dark glasses to the supermarket—or standing at the end of the produce aisle and yelling, "You can stop following me now, because I'm not going anywhere near the Budweiser display!"

Don't get me wrong. I have learned to live and live well with the occupational hazards of the ministry. And, although I once believed the myth of "play the role of the cute little cherub and you'll get by," I am no longer even slightly interested in just getting by. For I know now that I can have more. I know that I can have the abundant life that Jesus promised to my husband's congregation, because He promised it to me, too. I now understand that. But I also understand that learning how to live with a minister and love it involves a daily, occasionally hysterical, always complicated process.

Granted, I will probably never manage to eradicate all of the ministry's occupational hazards; but I now feel capable of taking the bad with the good. Most of the time, I can even do this without going off the deep end (i.e. staging a sleep-in to protest the Easter sunrise service or breaking out in a rash every time I get near a church). Yes, I am willing to run the obstacle course, but it is only because I have found out that I really do like the finish line. Or, as one minister's wife put it, "The joys outnumber the problems, but the problems are very real." Of course, God never promised rose gardens to his people anyway. Instead, he promised us his love and his presence; and, little by little, I have been discovering that this is more than enough after all.

So, I continue to struggle, to toil, to learn. I find myself becoming less the impeccable silhouette of a minister's wife and more the flesh-and-blood woman I was meant to be. I still spend quite a bit of time praying, "Pardon my King James, God; but I really do love you," but I think I am finally beginning to make the role work for me. Furthermore, I am also convinced that I am not the only minister's wife who has ever tried to take responsibility for her own life. In fact, I have been meeting all sorts of ministers' wives who have already learned how to cope with the outdated stereotypes and day-to-day complexities involved in the ministry.

Turning the Tide: Punching the Final Time Clock

Not surprisingly, most of the ministers' wives who are enjoying their lives are also the ministers' wives who have developed the knack of turning negatives into positives. For example, a large number of the ministers' wives I interviewed cited excessive demands on time as the most negative aspect of the ministry. One woman explained that she and her husband are never able to say, "Whew! Finished!" And another added that her pet peeve is the fact that people call on her husband's day off to take care of church business that could easily be dealt with on other days of the week. (The old "Where's the candelabra for next spring's wedding?" antic.) But many of those ministers' wives, through a combination of positive attitude and persistent action, are actually able to make the clock work for them, rather than against them.

Take, for instance, the minister's wife who said that she really enjoys traveling and attending seminars with her husband. Or the minister's wife who explained that she thinks of her life as fast-paced, varied, and rarely boring.

Several women even reported that they and their husbands are now working together to handle the time problem more successfully than ever before—and that their spouses (who used to spend every day at church and then moonlight as parish night watchmen) are now shepherding their flocks by letting the sheep do some of the work. So, although the negative time problem does exist, there are those ministers' wives who have found ways to add a few positive elements into the mix.

Turning the Tide: Recognizing "Unconstructive" Criticism

The second most common complaint voiced by the ministers' wives who were interviewed is the problem of being watched, pressured, and criticized; and the ministers' wives who have turned this negative into a positive have simply learned not to worry so much about what people think. "Our people generally accept us, mistakes and all, without being judgmental or condemnatory," an Illinois minister's wife reported, "and those who couldn't have found another church." Such thinking can undoubtedly go a long way toward smoothing one's path in life. And yet, most ministers' wives do admit that it isn't easy to contend with the task of dealing effectively and lovingly with all kinds of people in all kinds of complex situations.

"I often find myself smiling and saying sweet nothings to people I don't think deserve it," said a minister's wife of many years, and lots of other ministers' wives alluded to the fact that they have to spend too much time with "people problems" and are not able to spend any time actually having fun with anyone. Ironically though, "the people" are cited by many women as both the best and the worst things about being a minister's wife. First, then, the reasons given for placing "people" on the minus side of the fence.

Turning the Tide: Probing into the People Problem

I imagine that just about any minister's wife could recall at least one instance when her entire role revolved around pouring coffee for troubled people—not only people with troubles of their own, but those who like to make trouble for everyone else. Many times, those people are the individuals who are having difficulties functioning in all areas of life and who, therefore, decide to try and exert their authority in the church. (No entrance exam.) One minister's wife said that these kinds of people always think they rate special attention, and she is just one among many women who know exactly what it is like to grin and bear a board member who keeps everyone bored or a trustee no one can really trust.

Of course, Christ does call us to love the unlovely and to love them all the way into the Kingdom. He does call us to reach inside people's hearts and pull out the reasons behind their silent cries for help. And so, the struggle for balance will probably always go on. The minister's wife will probably always continue to feel it necessary to walk the tightrope between being selfish and allowing herself to be used so fully that there is nothing left to give. This sort of thing just seems to go with the territory.

On the positive side of the people issue, ministers' wives talk about sharing their lives with others and about being given the privilege of sharing with people in their most authentic moments—their highest joys and their deepest sorrows—the idea of the minister's wife as a part of the true essence of humanity. Some ministers' wives even say that they have "best friends" in their own churches and that no one has ever accused them of favoritism or toilet-papered their homes because of it.

Lots of ministers' wives also talk about the special kinds of fulfillment they get from being a part of their church people. "Those Sunday mornings when someone accepts Jesus Christ as Savior make it all worthwhile," said a minister's wife from Toledo, and she speaks for many others, too. For, although being deeply involved in the people business isn't always heart-warming enough to warm an empty bed at night, sometimes, in a way, it really is. And maybe the key to happiness in the manse is found in learning to celebrate those times.

At any rate, most ministers' wives do say that much of life in a people-oriented occupation depends upon the way you look at it, and I couldn't agree more. I would add, too, that there are only two basic ways of looking at people. The first is the way of the world. ("Joe? Yes, he may seem to be a nice person, but . . .") The second is the way of Christ. ("Joe? Yes, he may seem to be a terrible person, but . . .") I already know too many people who are caught in the trap of looking at everyone in the first way. God always looks deeper though. He always looks clear inside even the worst of people and pulls out something good, something that can be sanctified.

This is why God was able to look at a stuttering Levite who had just spent forty years working with a bunch of sheep and see an earthshaking spokesman for an entire nation of people. And, it is why Jesus could look at a man who was persecuting Christians and see the greatest apostle for Christ who ever lived. In a similar fashion, many people in many churches have been able to achieve great things for God merely because someone (maybe even some minister's wife) believed in them. Working with people—a minus that is also a very important plus.

Turning the Tide: Changing Dollars into Sense

Among the other less-than-perfect aspects of life in the ministry is the often-mentioned salary level. But many ministers' wives are able to come to terms with their husbands' paychecks successfully simply by concentrating on the good things in life. One minister's wife, for example, explained that a parsonage may be "simple, due to economic circumstance, but always full of books, the best magazines, and good music, as well as interesting people."

Many other ministers' wives are also able to look beyond the material side of life and identify with the minister's wife of forty-eight years who said, "I never could have nice things and the lovely home I dreamed of. How unimportant that seems now!" Some women are even able to laugh about their financial situations, often repeating the old story about how you don't make much money working for God, but you can't top the ultimate retirement plan. And therein, once again, lies one of life's most crucial keys—the sense of humor.

Laughing All the Way to the Manse

Ministers' wives who use their sense of humor to cope with the occupational hazards of the ministry are quick to explain that it really does help. "We laugh about people checking up on us," one minister's wife said, and I can understand how this can make being watched much less frustrating. In fact, I have often thought about making a game of the minister-watching pastime and taking my curious friends on a merry chase through some of the seamier parts of town. Especially on those days when I have fielded ten different unsolicited opinions on what color to paint my husband's office walls ("because you have to think of something that will suit the ministers to come after him").

Some clergy couples even use their sense of humor to communicate. "All right," they begin, "who is going to do the preaching at home tonight?" And then they decide. They decide, also, to have fun "in spite of it all"—in spite of the fact that Mrs. Jones told the members of her Bible study group that no self-respecting minister's wife would let her son drink pop in the fifth grade choir room (and besides, he is bound to get so many cavities that the minister will end up wanting a higher salary to pay the orthodontist's bills)—even in spite of the fact that Mrs. Jones caught the minister pinching his wife's posterior in the baptismal room and announced that everyone would be told about the preacher's muddied moral waters.

Looking Deeper

Thus, the basic idea in all of this is to "accentuate the positive" even if you can't eliminate all of the negatives. And a minister's wife can begin putting this idea into practice by spending less time thinking about the patriarch who stopped tithing when the minister "forgot" to visit him in the hospital during his hemorrhoidectomy (even though the mix-up was caused by the hospital computer) and more time thinking about all of the unique, God-given opportunities for Christian service that a woman receives just because she is a minister's wife.

One minister's wife told me the story of how she and her husband were handed a large amount of money one Christmas Eve and told to help someone. "Keep it until next Christmas," 'the minister said. "We've already taken care of everyone this year."

"You'll think of someone," the wise donor replied, and they did. Later that Christmas Eve night they carried all sorts of toys, food, and decorations down a path to a shabby old house. As soon as they knocked on the door, a woman opened it and greeted them with the words, "We knew you'd come."

"We didn't know we would go there," the minister's wife said, "but I guess God did." And the joy on the faces of people like those on that Christmas Eve lingers in a person's mind and heart far longer than a hundred negative statements ever could.

Even the problems that seem truly impossible to solve always become dimmer in view of the fact that, in Christ, we actually do have the means to work anything out. For, the Christian life really is more than a nice little fairy tale; and the concepts of spiritual growth, powerful prayer, and God in control really are more than the elements of a stale old three-point sermon. That which we are preaching is real, as real as it comes, even for the minister and his wife. It is just that putting God first is sometimes more complicated for the clergy couple because it isn't always the same as putting a church meeting first.

Things also seem more complicated on those days when work seems so fruitless, and there certainly are days when I feel that my efforts are totally worthless. But whenever I feel like that, whenever no one cares about the three hours I spent preparing my Church School lesson, for example, or whenever the children in my church study group start taking bets on which day they will finally be able to force my resignation as their teacher, I have found that it helps to call time-out and spend a few minutes thinking about little Bill.

Dear Bill . . .

Little Bill—without a doubt the most aggressive, trouble-making junior high choir member ever to set foot in our church. Today Bill is not little anymore. He is very grown up, and he is an extremely capable Minister of Music. (When he got his first church, I thought about writing him a good-luck note and telling him that God would probably get even with him by sending fifty unmanageable junior high students to his first choir practice.) Yes, I guess one can never know what the end results of his work will be, and thinking about Bill truly does help. In fact, lately I have been thinking about writing to Bill and thanking him—but I'm not exactly sure what I want to thank him for. . . .

And yet, Bill or no Bill, there are times when clergy couples do get bogged down in the ministry's negatives. Sometimes this happens because we hesitate to stand behind our roles and/or our convictions (even if everyone else in the world *does* believe that the minister's wife should force her fifteen-year-old son to attend the weekly men's prayer breakfast—and to cut his hair before he does). Other times, we have trouble because we refuse to make the adjustments that need to be made.

Doris Halverson said it this way:

> In the Fourth Presbyterian Church in Washington, D.C., we know many prominent men, and most of us don't begin to realize the adjustments their wives have to make. Even the prominent leaders themselves have to be subject to whatever tasks they have before them. Submission is not a bad word. Now that I am a grandmother, ready to retire, it is a thrill and bonus to have raised three wonderful children, all of whom are in the church and love the Lord. And it is great to have the satisfaction of knowing I have supported a man who has been faithful to the Word of God. How grateful you are when you have lived a life that has served a worthy cause.

A life with purpose. I certainly want to live a life like that. I want to live a full life and a joyful life, a life that will be a good example for all those poor, unsuspecting young females who will someday marry handsome, smooth-talking seminarians (and then find out that a minister's undershirts get as dirty as anyone else's). In fact, I don't want even one of those women to end up burying her personality under a pile of coffee grounds because of me. I want, instead, to show both the prospective and the disillusioned ministers' wives that there really is life after marriage to a minister. I want to show them that it can be a good life too, because I truly believe it can be.

Today's Emerging Minister's Wife

Yes, I think that the life of a minister's wife can be a fantastic, exciting, satisfying, even fun-filled life; and I am not the only one who thinks so. Karen Mains, for example, talks about how wonderful it is to be married to a man whose priority is the Kingdom of God. "David has always been the spiritual head in that he has always been centrally concerned with the supernatural," she explained. "He is a man of prayer and a lover of studying the Word. This is a rare privilege for a wife." And, an Ohio minister's wife added, "There is something so stimulating about having a happy husband, and I am married to a baseball nut who loves his work so much that he wouldn't trade places with the owner of the Cincinnati Reds."

It may not always seem to be the case, but there really are many happy ministers' wives in our world today. Of course, most of them are happy mainly because they have carved out their own unique paths in life. Take, for instance, the Baptist minister's wife who spends a lot of time taking care of her home and family. She said that she truly enjoys making church a fun place to be, and teaching children that the Christian lifestyle does make sense. A second minister's wife has chosen a different approach to life, for she is in the process of advancing in her career. She, too, enjoys her life in the church—so much, in fact, that she said she honestly had trouble answering my questions about the negative side of the ministry.

A third woman, who has been married to her minister for almost fifty years, has always spent time pursuing various interests (political issues, community work, interracial concerns) outside the local church. She said that she "can't imagine a life that could be happier or more fulfilling than that of a minister's wife." And a fourth minister's wife, who thinks of herself as a partner in her husband's ministry, finds her kind of life to be filled with a great deal of satisfaction. "I wouldn't trade it for anything," she said.

Four ministers' wives. All very different, all very happy, all doing their "own things." Not one of them would be happy with the other's life, but each one has an integral slot to fill in the body of Christ. All of them have been accepted and affirmed by the churches in which they serve, although they have probably worked very hard to get to that place in life. For, they are undoubtedly women who have searched for their own special niches in life—and have found them—in the assurance that the right to do so is one of the highest compliments God gives to his children. Four ministers' wives. All very different. All coping successfully with the rapidly changing world around them.

Beyond the Stereotypes

How are the rest of us doing? Is the world zipping by too quickly for some of us? Do *we* who are ministers' wives honestly know where the church fits into it all? Do we know where we fit into the church, and do we know how to explain all of this to our congregations? How many of us are still trying to decide whether or not to let our daughters wear slacks to school while the rest of the people in the world are asking crucial questions about the very essence of sexuality itself, questions like "What is male?" and "What is female?"

How many of us are truly willing to grow, in spite of all the obstacles, and in the knowledge that peoples' feelings about themselves do change with each new stage in life? Are we remaining silent often enough to hear what God has to say to us about living in today's world? Are we speaking out often enough to be heard by the people who need to hear us? How many of us are being flexible enough to reach people and, at the same time, courageous enough to hold tight to that which is real and unchanging?

What really is happening behind the scenes in the parsonage today? It depends, I think. Some of the clergy couples inside those manses are still serving cinnamon rolls baked according to great grandmother's recipe, but many of them are baking the rolls together now. Other clergy couples have thrown out all the old recipes and are heading for work in opposite directions each morning, but numbers of these people are coming together again at night for the first time in their married lives. Still others are splitting up; but, even then, many of the rest of us are learning some important lessons about understanding and empathy and forgiveness from them.

It is clear that the things that are happening in the parsonage today are both bitter and sweet. And, whatever else can be said about all of this, today's clergy couples are having quite an effect on all of society. People everywhere are watching and waiting and wondering. Some of those people are afraid that their churches may be selling out to the world, while others believe that the end results of openness and honesty are always good. A third (and very large) group of people, however, are not sure what to think, simply because the church has never been a viable option for them. It was always "too remote" or they were never "good enough to be Christians." They didn't "fit in" . . . and I can't help but think how wonderful it would be if we who are members of today's clergy families could use our own imperfections as tools to reach out to those people. Perhaps we could even turn our own struggles and our own pain into real healing, not only for ourselves, but for others, too. Perhaps.

Toward the Milk and Honey

I know I am ending this book with a lot of questions. But it is because I believe that the answers to those questions lie within each one of us—somewhere behind those feelings of inadequacy and resentment and frustration—somewhere deep inside, in that part of a human being that is capable of communing one-to-one with God. This book, therefore, must end on a note of reaffirmation, not of the minister's wife, but of the power of God within her. And I must ask one final question, a question that a friend of mine once brought to my attention: Why *would* any talented young man in his right mind, a man with unlimited opportunities (a man like my husband), ever choose the ministry in the first place?

Most ministers' wives, at one time or another, have asked themselves that question. Some of us have even felt tempted to conclude that our husbands were never in their right minds to begin with. The correct answer, though, is that he wouldn't. That man wouldn't choose the ministry. Not because there is anything wrong or right about his mental state, but because, as my friend put it, left alone we would all make other choices. "You did not choose me"; said Jesus, "I chose you." And, he also said, "... I am with you always, ..." Yes, the world may continue to think that we who "choose" the clergy life are not in our right minds, but at least each clergy couple can know differently. At least each minister's wife can build her own life in the shelter—and in the peace—of that truth. And that is probably not such a bad place to start after all.

Moral :

A wise minister's wife will learn how to find the thorns in her rose garden before they find her.

Epilogue

I married a minister, and then I began waiting for the future to arrive. "Just until I learn how to make coffee, God," I said. "Or just until the offerings pick up and we can buy that sofa bed, or just until I can get some of it right." Then one day I realized that my future is here. It is now. Today really is the best possible time for each one of us to begin, finally, to live.